VIKING
WEAPONS & WARFARE

VIKING
WEAPONS & WARFARE

J. Kim Siddorn

TEMPUS

First published 2000

PUBLISHED IN THE UNITED KINGDOM BY:

Tempus Publishing Ltd
The Mill, Brimscombe Port
Stroud, Gloucestershire GL5 2QG

PUBLISHED IN THE UNITED STATES OF AMERICA BY:

Tempus Publishing Inc.
2 Cumberland Street
Charleston, SC 29401
1-888-313-2665

Tempus books are available in France and Germany
from the following addresses:

Tempus Publishing Group   Tempus Publishing Group
21 Avenue de la République   Gustav-Adolf-Straße 3
37300 Joué-lès-Tours   99084 Erfurt
FRANCE   GERMANY

British Library Cataloguing in Publication Data.
A catalogue record for this book is available from the British Library.

ISBN 0 7524 1419 4

Typesetting and origination by Tempus Publishing.
PRINTED AND BOUND IN GREAT BRITAIN

Contents

*This book is dedicated to all these people
because they made me think about what I was doing*

*Those who wore fur wrapped around their legs
The man who owned the sword called Budgie
Those who wore chrome studs and black leather
Those who wore their Doc Martens in costume
The man in red with the worst sword in the world
The few brave souls who wore horns on their helmets*

*The man who walked barefoot across York in the snow
Those who upheld the Law and those who hid behind it
Vigdis the Bear who kissed the keel of a Longship
The hewers of wood and fetchers of water
The man who didn't steal the Black Tern
Those who believed it was all worth it*

Wayne Hill and Steve Hurley who died with their boots on

Oh, and Geoff Davies, who taught me a lot more than he intended

List of illustrations

Text figures

Colour plates

Preface

When asked to write this book, I welcomed the opportunity to propound some theories, speak of my first-hand experience and forward the lifelong interest I've had in what we all used to call the Dark Ages — before it became unfashionable so to do. I have therefore set out what I know of this most fascinating era for the re-enactor, the academic and the general reader in an accessible way.

For the better part of 20 years I have been a working re-enactor. When I started in 1980 there was no living history, just combatants and the second-class citizens called non-combatants who sat glumly between the ropes whilst we warriors trod the field of slaughter, sword in hand. It was a simpler, more direct time and I take this small opportunity to greet those few who remember it. Farr Heil!

It was also a time of dearth. If you wanted something re-creating you could do it yourself and learn by your mistakes or pay someone else to learn by theirs. I am of a practical turn of mind and at one time or another have made more swords, spears and shoes than I care now to count. Although the bulk were made with modern tools, I always took the opportunity to make at least one of everything by hand. This gave me an invaluable insight into the time and effort that it takes to get something done without power tools — but I still had electric light after dark and was not exhausted from a day's ploughing.

All this activity required time and I found that re-enactment was no longer a hobby but a way of life and then a much-loved honorary job. For about 14 years now I have been the national organiser of Regia Anglorum, the UK's foremost society dealing with this period of history. Regia recreates the life and times of the folk who lived in and around the Islands of Britain from the time of King Alfred to the First Crusade, Vikings, Saxons, Cymru and Normans. We attempt to do so with as much accuracy as possible and have attained an international reputation for authenticity of costume, equipment and portrayal. This attitude must be paid for, I'm afraid: in line with continuing research, the D-section pouch and long, dangly strap end have now vanished from the costume you see me wearing in the above photo, taken only five months before I wrote this. I would not like to count the number of articles that have gone this way, but it is the price we are all prepared to pay to attain and maintain high standards.

Despite all the advice and teaching, there are still places where myself and others disagree, and in any work that deals with thousand-year-old artefacts there will be areas of doubt. The opinions and suppositions expressed in this book are those of the author — as are the errors.

Kim Siddorn, October 2000

Acknowledgements

Since the end of the 1970s Viking Age re-enactment has been an important feature of my life and from the constant interaction of Society life, I have learned a huge amount from the membership. It would be invidious to mention some when I cannot mention all and I simply take this opportunity to extend my appreciation to all those who have brought something to this work.

Regia Anglorum maintains a huge photographic library and in exchange for this credit have supplied almost all the colour photographs used in this book. Individual photos are credited where this is not the case. The bulk of them are the work of that fine photographer and cameraman Ken Guest. My grateful thanks to Regia for the kind use of their copyright material.

The great majority of the line drawings in the text are the work of my dear friend Roland Williamson who has been a re-enactor for a year longer than me. He has also contributed to the content and corrected errors where appropriate. Dave McDermott used his skill upon the text and stopped up holes through which grammar and punctuation were escaping. We have done our best to track down the originators of any other artwork included, but I should especially mention Colin and Ben Levick who have given me permission to use some of their work.

When I came to look at shields and scabbards, I chanced upon the excellent work of Peter Beatson. Realising that it would be foolish to cover the same ground, we arrived at an amicable arrangement and much of those chapters are his work.

My thanks to these people in particular and to the many that have managed to keep me abreast of recent work, some of it yet unpublished, and have kept me from making too much of a fool of myself.

Finally, trite though it may be, I must mention my wife Hazel. Without her active support and tacit backing, I could not have lived the last 20 years of my life in the way that I have. It is, quite simply, a debt of gratitude that neither I nor those who have willingly followed me down this rocky path can ever repay. To Hazel, Roland and the members of Regia Anglorum, I extend my fond and heartfelt thanks and appreciation.

Introduction

For as long as I can remember I have been interested in the people we call the Vikings. It is even too long ago for me to recall the reason, but I know I am not alone, for people all over the world know of these fierce sea-raiders who erupted out of Scandinavia over 1200 years ago. Considering there were never many of them — perhaps no more than 100,000 at any one time — they left a mark upon the history of northern Europe out of all proportion to their importance in the wider context. The man on the Clapham omnibus may not now even know the date of the Battle of Hastings, but he will have heard of the Vikings, complete with double-headed axe, furry leggings and horned helmet.

Sadly, very little of what our bus passenger 'knows' is even vaguely accurate. A Viking warrior would have turned the furry leggings into gloves, cut one blade off the axe to make it lighter and faster and removed the dangerous horns (more of which anon) to make them into the far more useful drinking vessels, combs and gaming pieces. He would have been embarrassed to find the bum-freezer tunic he'd been wished into was two feet too short, his shaggy furry cloak only useful for sleeping under and would have immediately combed and cut his voluminous hair and beard.

As far as we can tell, this image we have of these people dates to the early performances of Wagner's *Ring Cycle* at Bayreuth in the late 1870s. This marks the first time that the modern re-enactor (who holds authenticity close to his heart) falls out violently with the professional Costume Designer. Would that it had been the last time . . . I have a copy of Snorri's *Hemskringla* that was printed in 1899 in Norway. Written in Old Icelandic, it contains woodcuts which show warriors in simple pointed helmets wearing long tunics and carrying big round shields and nine-foot spears. Quite heartening really.

In this book, there are various descriptive terms used and these fall generally in line with current popular practice. The 'Fall of Rome in the West' refers to AD 410 when the last of the Legions left Britannia. 'The Dark Ages' used to be a bit of a catchall and some took it as ending in AD 1066. However, we know so much more about Anglo-Saxon England and Europe at that time than we did 20 years ago that the boundaries keep on rolling back almost year by year. For myself, I now take this term to mean AD 410 to 650, also eloquently referred to as the time of the 'English Settlements'. From here, the term in common use is 'Early Medieval Times' which takes us to the Battle of Hastings and beyond. I personally use the term 'The Viking Age' to refer to the period of the Viking raids on Britain — AD 793 to AD 1066 — which started with the raid on Lindisfarne and ended when Harold Godwinsson broke the power of Scandinavian arms in the West at the battle of Stamford Bridge.

It has become the politically correct view in the last ten years to portray the Vikings as mainly peaceful traders and settlers. If I had spent a year and the equivalent of hundreds of thousands of pounds on a Drakkar, I am certain I would fill it with the most bloodthirsty, well-equipped, weapon-handy men I could find — arrogant and cynical fellows intent on making their mark on their enemies. I quote from something I once heard Magnus Magnusson say in the late 1970s: 'I am not a Viking apologist. In a bloodthirsty age they were more bloodthirsty than most.' This is a view to which I unswervingly adhere.

My efforts do not set out to portray any particular attitude, but I do feel that we do our ancestors a distinct disservice if we try to judge them with modern eyes since our life experience is radically different. The man who leapt off the ship's prow a thousand years ago got his feet just as wet as mine, but I have an expectation of a warm bed that night. Further, it is a mistake to look down upon those who lived in a past time as being lesser than us in some way — but it is an error we all make, myself included. They were capable of just as much happiness, misery, gluttony, abstinence, compassion, cruelty, cynicism, greed, lust and sheer bloody-mindedness as we are today. They were also great pragmatists. There is a particularly excellent little saying of Scandinavian derivation that always makes me smile: 'These three things are hard to talk to, a king bent on conquest, a Viking in his war gear and a low-born man protected by patronage.'

Much of what I know of the use of the arms and armour has come from first-hand experience as a weapon smith and combatant re-enactor and this may certainly provide a subjective interpretation. However, I have never been a member of the armed forces of this or any other nation and I do not have (thank God) any first-hand experience of people trying to kill me — but there have been times when it really felt like they were — and that, of course, is why we all do it. The living moment that joins us to the lives of our ancestors so long dead — that rare, unforgettable moment when the gunwale of the ship dips into the sea and 50 gallons of Baltic rushes aboard; when the shield wall collapses and shouting men run you down; when you roll out of bed to pull your soggy turn shoes on for the fifth day in succession — and it comes to you: 'it must have been just like this!'.

Remember

The spring came upon the land. From it's stable, the black ship was drawn,
that steed of the sea-spray.
As the birch-buds quickened, ropes were laid and cloth was sewn.
In the bright morning the ship strode forth upon its legs until
the fair north wind blew. Then wind-catcher spread her wings
and flew across the salt road, clove the whale's way, salt spray
at the prow of the sea-strider. Forward pressed the reed-spreaders
as the sons of Odinn lifted their battle-boards from the edge
of the sea's serpent. Bereft of scales, it lay listless at the river's rim.
Forward went the men to battle, the touch of their war-nets
cold comfort at neck and elbow. Bright were the battle-hardened
blades as they arced in the day's light. Fearsome were the foes
that took and gave crafty wounds.

Now were the men marred, bright hair in the dirt,
wounds darkening and death bringing.

At the hearth's side, brave tales were told, the dead living
on in men's minds as they sit in the hall of the
One-Eyed Raven Feeder.
Ale and strong mead were drunk, but the arm's of many
a man's good wife lay cold and unfilled.
Salt crusted, the bow of the sea-strider waited for memory to fade.

1 The havoc of heathen men

Ann. DCCXCIII: In this year dire forewarnings
came over the land of the Northumbrians
and miserably terrified the people: these were extraordinary
whirlwinds and lightnings,
and fiery dragons were seen flying in the air.
A great famine soon followed these omens;
and soon after that, in the same year, on the sixth
of the ides of Ianr,
the havoc of heathen men miserably destroyed
God's church on Lindisfarne,
through rapine and slaughter.

Anglo-Saxon Chronicle

As Rome fought great battles along the Rhine and lost whole legions in the darkling
Teutoberg forest, a people-group made their way into a sparsely settled land. Cold,
inhospitable and with a short growing season, it seemed an unlikely place to generate
sufficient spare resources to enable a few generations of men to develop an ocean-going
ship from a curious assembly of planks and ropes in which you or I would not cross a
boating lake. Yet that is what happened: as continental influences and migration from the
east caused the cultural changes that led from the Vendal culture to the people we have

1 Norse raider equipped for battle

come to call the Vikings, the interaction of cultures seems to have accelerated developments in boat technology. Finds such as the Bjorke and Nydam Boats from the first three centuries of the first millennium AD show a developing theme based upon log boat construction. From this unlikely beginning developed a particular line of sailing vessels which could attempt ocean voyages across the Atlantic and — at the other extreme — light craft which could deal with shallow, fast-flowing rivers and were capable of being moved across land to another river or lake.

Their skills in developing iron-founding techniques made iron more available in Scandinavia, allowing them to clear forest more quickly and plough heavier soils. Within 300 years, the population grew too large for the limited area available as living space, and with their ship technology they were able to expand 'to see the land of strangers, far away'.

As a West Germanic people, only free men in Norse society were allowed to bear arms and this right was fiercely guarded. The weapon more frequently used than any other was the spear and the great majority of appropriate grave-finds contain a spear of one kind or another. In many ways, the spear and its use in the killing of men — and, thereby, the

2 Saxon Thegn properly equipped for service
in the Fyrd (Levick)

defence of hearth and home — had a fundamental effect on all of the West Germanic warrior peoples and it appears again and again in literature as representing more than a stick with an iron blade at one end. Odin is pierced by the spear in his search for knowledge, something that settled into the mindset of Viking warriors and remained there during their conversion to Christianity. Christ, after all, was sacrificed on a cross of wood and pierced by a spear in his last extremity.

The sword was reserved for the wealthy and the professional warrior — by reason of cost and availability if nothing else. The scramsaex in all its forms was also used in warfare, although to a lesser extent, and the Vikings appear to have liked to use the short-hafted axe in battle. Bladed weapons such as swords, knives etc. were always enclosed in a scabbard when not in use.

Although skill with the bow was much admired and the weapon was certainly used in battle, the universal use of large wooden shields seems to have largely discouraged its use

3 Much inshore work would have been pursued by rowing

as a weapon of mass destruction. The sling was also in use throughout the period, although the same restrictions must have applied to that weapon as the bow.

Few men could have afforded to wear an iron helmet in battle, but I have no doubt that hardened leather helmets were used at the least and anything that would protect the vulnerable head could have been pressed into service — perhaps wickerwork and wood were used or layers of coarse linen or heavy felt, although they leave little mark in the archaeological record.

Linen and wool would have formed the basis for padded body armour, worn by the ordinary warrior as a primary defence and as a good foundation for mail by his richer compatriots. An inch or two of firmly stuffed padded jack below the mail protects you well and is easy and cheap to make in the long winter evenings.

The mail shirt was very much the mark of the professional warrior and a byrnie was much sought after. Mail was also used as a neck curtain on helmets and might well have found its way onto the backs of gloves if they were worn.

The shield, the warrior's friend, was a safe haven in the hurly-burly of battle. Made of wood and covered with cloth or leather, all those who went to war in those days took at least one shield with them. Its use had a fundamental effect on the employment of weapons and the tactics of warfare, particularly in respect of the use of the spear.

Finally, without the ship that they developed, there would have been no Viking Age. Europe would have evolved along quite different paths and the spur towards national defence would not have developed at that time. One could speculate that Rollo Rognvaldsson (so tall that he was called 'Hrolf' meaning 'the Ganger' or 'Walker') would never have gone to the King of France and asked for the northern part of his country in AD 911. No Normandy, no Norman Conquest. One might speculate that trade would have been slower, language more regional, ideas more traditional, society more tribal.

Without intending it, the Vikings inflicted on their European neighbours a reason to band together for defence, to support national armies and policies and to evolve systems of training and weapons production that once in place were not to be dismantled. I think it is no stretch of the imagination to say that we owe them the seeds of our national identity, forcing us as they did to fight off a common enemy.

2 Iron

Trust no man for the best of friends may be false in their heart.
Trust no woman, for women are strange fey creatures and
no man can know them.
Trust no horse or dog: they are living things and
follow their spirit.
Trust nothing you can buy. That which is bought
may be sold again.
Trust not the weather, for a smiling dawn may be
a fearful storm by noon.
But iron, this you can trust. The strength of the mountain's
root is in it,
It holds the secret of the fire in its heart —
clean, bright and deadly.

Attributed to Attila the Hun

After the first discovery of iron in the Fertile Crescent the secret spread slowly north. It was a tremendous discovery initially and Tutankhamun's royal mummy was entombed in 1340 BC with an iron-bladed dagger, then more precious than gold. Ore sources were not much looked for and meteoric iron was a major source in the very early days, in itself an indication of its rarity. Early Iron Age blades of almost pure iron might be work-hardened to some extent by skilful pounding with a smith's hammer.

This would compact the material, but fatigue factors set in and lead to brittleness. Early swords in iron were certainly no better (and frequently worse) than the highly-developed

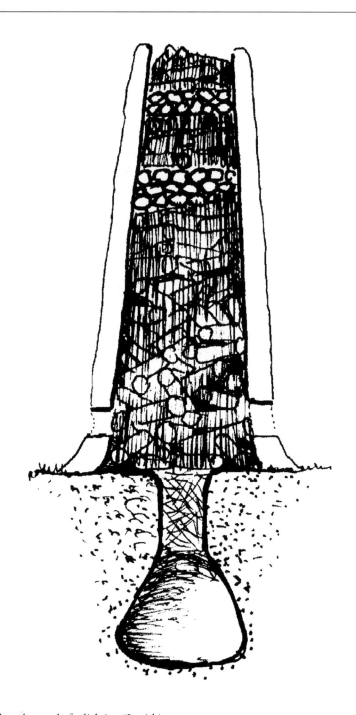

4   *The filled smelter ready for lighting (Levick)*

5   *Keeping it going (Levick)*

Bronze Age blades which they sought to supersede. As the technology evolved to deal with the new product, it became common knowledge that iron ore is relatively plentiful as opposed to copper and tin which were both uncommon and widely dispersed. If trade in either metal was interrupted, bronze could not be manufactured. However, although more difficult to work, iron needed no second element to make it into a useable material apart from charcoal. This could be readily manufactured in the vast forests that covered much of Europe.

Whilst I hesitate to use the outmoded word 'Celt' in this or any other context, it is a useful literary shorthand to describe the group of Late Bronze Age and Iron Age cultures that lived in Europe in the early days of Rome's greatness. They were great technicians, inventors and developers and their bronze casting and working techniques have never been bettered whilst using the methods available to them. The great bulk of the early knowledge of working in iron comes from centuries of their hard work and trial-and-error experimentation. Contact with these people, often viewed as barbarians by the Greeks and Romans — 'Celt' comes from the Greek 'Keltoi', meaning 'Trouser wearer' — refined the Romans' techniques in the early days of Empire. It was the Celts who invented the wire drawing technology required to make the raw material for chain mail, the Romans adopting the idea somewhere around 100 BC and subsequently spreading it across the known world as the Empire grew.

From before the days of the Empire until long after the Viking Age, the only method available for extracting iron from ore was by the use of a bloomery furnace. The ore would be broken into small fragments, washed, and pre-roasted to remove the water. The earliest

6   Forcing the fire (Levick)

furnaces were simply a bowl-shaped hollow in the ground filled with charcoal and ore. From this developed the shaft furnace, a truncated cone around 1m high with a hollow cut under one side. This would be filled with a layered and partially mixed body consisting of hardwood charcoal and crushed iron ore. The ore might itself be a mixed supply of high and low grade ores and that ancient standby, limonite, or 'bog iron'.

This strange substance is precipitated out of iron-rich water by bacteriological action in the depths of peat bogs and can actually be raked out of shallow, peaty lake beds. Although impure, it is easier than mining! Once reduced to small, thin plaques, it is possible to hammer weld it into usable blades without further ado, but the phosphorous content tended to make it too brittle. Undisturbed, the bog will rebuild its supply within about 20 years. As iron came from bogs, it was frequently returned there and Celtic communities often made sacrifices of captured weapons and other iron objects in these soggy and mysterious places.

The furnace might be naturally drafted by means of the wind or constantly bellowed during firing. The plan was to supply the air at a high enough rate, raising the internal temperature enough to reduce the ore to a mass of metal and slag and remove impurities such as sulphur, phosphorus and arsenic. If the furnace has been loaded correctly and the burn managed with care and skill, the carbon in the charcoal will cause the iron to form a number of small, massy lumps which tend to flow together in the heat of the fire — although it is important to understand that the iron never truly melts unless there is limestone included in the mix. This is caused by the iron oxide being consumed in the reducing conditions of the fire and changed to carbon monoxide. Some impurities will burn away and others will melt as slag (taking a lot of iron with them!), which liquefies and runs out of the bottom of the furnace. When the moment is judged to be correct, the fire is covered to exclude the air and the fire is allowed to go out.

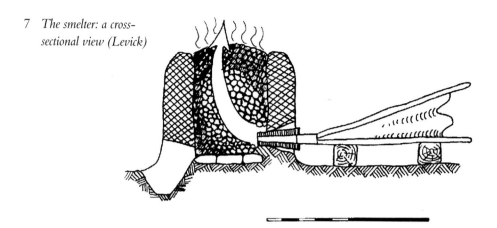

7   *The smelter: a cross-sectional view (Levick)*

In the lower part of the furnace lurks the product of all these labours, a craggy, rough and heavy mass of red-hot material consisting mainly of iron mixed with some silica, called a bloom. Depending on the design of the furnace, this can either be dragged out of the draft hole, out of the top or, in some cases, by breaking up the walls. As the science of iron production gathered pace, it was discovered (probably by the purest chance) that the process could be improved by the addition of a certain amount of limestone to the mix. At smelting temperatures, limestone acts as a flux and also raises the internal temperature by a few degrees by chemical action, a useful characteristic in moderation, producing a cleaner bloom.

This bloom might weigh anything from a few grammes to 30 or 40kg and it is here that the hard work begins, for it must be 'wrought', that is, reduced by hammering, twisting, folding and squeezing in an attempt to remove as much as possible of the slag, ash and other impurities that have appeared during firing. If it has been a good day and all has gone well, then the result at this stage will be a bar of wrought iron. It is clean and grey in colour, does not rust much and is ideal for making cauldrons, tripods, chains, helmets, shield bosses and thin bars for drawing into wire. Unfortunately, as for swords, it would make a poor weapon, being easily bent and distorted and incapable of holding much of an edge.

If there was too much air admitted to the burn, too much charcoal added to the fill (or equally likely, too much time was spent over lunch), the temperature may have risen too high and unexpected amounts of carbon will have been absorbed by the iron — and then the bloom may be flawed. Instead of a roughly consistent mass of fairly soft iron, the carbon will have produced places in the mass where the material has become what we call today 'cast' iron. Invisible to the naked eye, these nodules will shatter on impact or stop the hammer dead in its tracks, a tooth-rattling experience for anyone who has experienced it. Alternatively, there will be great voids in the bloom where the cast iron has melted away into the slag.

Between wrought and cast iron lies 'hard' iron, the medieval name for a metal we might refer to as steel, although there were some differences that would give a metallurgist pause for thought. It looked different and, having a higher carbon content, worked differently from wrought iron. All other things being equal, the more carbon there is in the iron, the more stiffly it will work. Unlike iron, the higher grades of steel could be hardened and tempered and it did not take that much carbon to produce a good cutting edge. Analysis of various finds shows that the cutting edges were not very hard by modern standards, but they were certainly an improvement on bronze. If the purchaser was prepared to pay more, a thin section of high-grade steel could be set into the cutting edge, giving a composite weapon or tool of great strength and durability. These composite iron implements were a great technical achievement as steel has a higher melt-temperature than the iron. Wrought iron enters the semi-liquid welding stage at about 1380°C and starts to burn at about 1530°C while the range for 100pt steel is between about 1222°C and 1440°C.

Naturally, the actual welding temperature depended on the exact constituents of the material and there was sometimes a plastic stage of only a few degrees where the two materials could be persuaded to join together by hammering them at welding temperatures. As the blade reaches welding temperature, a few sparks will fly up from the iron that indicate it is just about to burn. This is the only warning given and preparation must be made to strike quickly and with great accuracy. 'Striking when the iron is hot' takes on its original meaning.

Iron in the North

The Norse people we call the Vikings lived in the Late Age, a time that is mutable as it depended on where you lived as to when it occurred. Iron was expensive, about as expensive as silver is to us today. Therefore, it was not thrown away, but scraps were hoarded and reused, either by being incorporated into fresh iron from the smelter by hammer welding, or by simply being forged into something else. Making tools from iron was hard, difficult work and once made, things appear to have been in service much longer than their modern equivalents. This goes a long way towards explaining why there are no helmet finds from Britain in this period and precious little mail either: they were simply reused until they wore away into rust and iron filings or, in the case of mail, were broken up when the shirt became too thin to wear any more, the remains being used at the backs of helmets.

Work-hardened iron does not really form a sound basis for weapon manufacture — but practice makes master, as they say. It was during the early days of Empire that Rome came to understand that ores from various sources might well have different properties. The finished metal benefited in terms of hardness and toughness from the occurrence of manganese, nickel and tungsten in these ores, with manganese especially adding to the ability to work harden the edge. It was not considered worthy of much comment, but these natural alloys were employed in tools, weapons or hardware according to their various virtues.

It has been suggested that there were up to seven different types of ferrous alloy were in use for weapon manufacture in the late Dark Ages and early medieval period. I am prepared to agree that such materials might have been available but I am far from certain that they were knowingly assembled and used with an expectation of a particular outcome.

I am inclined to the opinion that virtually all swords were made from either wrought iron or wrought iron modified by working it into a higher grade of steel resulting in simple and complex laminated welding. Wrought iron is usually very low in carbon. A high carbon content is what distinguishes steel from wrought iron.

The three basic ferrous compounds that a smith had to work with were as follows:
Wrought iron might vary from containing perhaps three per cent silica from slag inclusion and other sources and virtually no carbon at all to containing about 0.04%. Such iron is referred to as having four points of carbon (0.04pts). This metal is very resistant to corrosion. (I have a Nelson's Navy cannonball which we have used as a doorstop since the mid 1970s. I cleaned it with a wire brush when I brought it into the house and it is still bright and shiny.) Wrought iron is also soft, malleable, welds well and does not readily burn during forging.

Steel covers the range from around 4pts to 225pts (2.25%) of included carbon, although most modern steels vary between 20pt 'mild steel' to 150pt 'tool steel'. Mild steel is about 0.01-0.4 per cent carbon, medium carbon steel is about 0.4 -0.7 per cent carbon, high carbon steel is 0.7 -1.1 per cent carbon and tool steel can have as much as 1.7 per cent. There are other components in modern steels such as chromium, nickel, manganese, tungsten etc. but when they occurred naturally in local iron ores that was either an advantage or problem depending on what our smith was trying to achieve. More susceptible to corrosion, steel is also harder, less malleable, more difficult to weld and more easily burnt in forging. As its carbon content increases, so the material tends more towards springiness. This characteristic means that it will also shatter when over-hardened and crack when worked at the wrong temperature, all in proportion to its carbon content. Steel has a low inclusion of silica and contains — either by ancient accident or modern design — various trace metals that modify the behaviour of the steel in use.

Cast iron has a typical carbon content of 35pts to 425pts, but carries a much higher degree of impurity that might include phosphorus, silica, arsenic or other materials. Its carbon content means that it will rust, but it is non-malleable, hard, brittle and heat resistant. Our Dark Age smiths must have loathed the sight of it. Although it takes well to fine-detail casting, transfers heat well and is excellent in compression, it was over 2000 years before we evolved the early modern engineering ability to deal with it and utilise it in quantity. To this day, most vehicle brake discs are made from cast iron.

Wrought iron was widely available in Europe in our period of interest, but cast iron was undesirable and was put back for re-working. Steels were uncommon and only produced from wrought iron by hammering, folding and twisting in an environment that promoted the inclusion of carbon into the iron. This can be achieved by packing wrought iron rods into an iron box filled with powdered charcoal and maintaining it at a high temperature for some considerable time. Some of the carbon would migrate into the iron, turning parts of it into steel. The same process of adding carbon is used today in case hardening, adding carbon to the metal's surface to increase hardness. This naturally led to the type of composite steel we refer to today as pattern welded steel. Of some 140+ swords from the fifth through tenth centuries discovered in England and X-rayed by the British Museum, over 60 per cent were pattern welded. This is explored more fully in the chapter about swords.

If one were fortunate in the availability of iron ores, one might be able to accumulate enough of the right type of steely iron to make a blade of uniform, homogenised metal. Chance, testing the product with a hard punch or simply long experience might also lead a smith to actually select ores from different sources and forge them into a sword so as to take advantage of their diverse properties. Swords of both types were in use throughout the early medieval period.

It might be worth pointing out in this section that Damascus steel is not manufactured by the smith but by the smelter, and — although it looks similar — is not made by pattern welding. More properly called Wootz or Crucible steel, it was imported from the east by the Romans and probably originated in India. Alternate layers of iron and carbon are placed carefully in a crucible and subjected to a long and complicated process of slow heating and cooling. When the process is completed, a cake of steel is retrieved from the bottom of the crucible and it is in this form that the 'Damascened' ingots were exported from India to the west, being traded through Damascus. In all likelihood, completed weapons were sold in the city too. The patterning in this steel is a lot more random than in pattern welding and is caused by a layering off in the smelter of different grades of steel and iron.

3 Spear

Do not go out into the fields without your spear
A man never knows when he will need one.

For nine whole nights I hung upon the tree,
Pierced by the spear, myself sacrificed to myself.

Halvamel

The spear was the principal weapon of the Viking age, used by wealthy karls and bondi and in Saxon England, from the fighting thegns who formed the bulk of the English aristocracy to the poorest freeman in the Fyrd. It was venerated and honoured above all others, sometimes including the sword.

In its simplest form, a spear is nothing more than a pointed stick. Ash is the best wood and was most frequently chosen because it naturally grows straight and is capable of withstanding a good hard knock without breaking. However hazel, field maple and some fruit woods have good characteristics and oak is strong if heavy and given to shattering occasionally. One can quickly sharpen one end by cutting or rubbing on a stone, harden the tip in a fire to char off the fluffy wood and converting the unburned timber into a hard, resilient point. It was with the spear in this form that our earliest ancestors first followed the northern ice, chasing the wild horse and using the weapon to kill the woolly mammoth in deadfalls. It would be foolish to say it is man's earliest weapon, but it must have been on the scene as a specific tool very early in our history.

8 *Various spear head designs (Levick)*

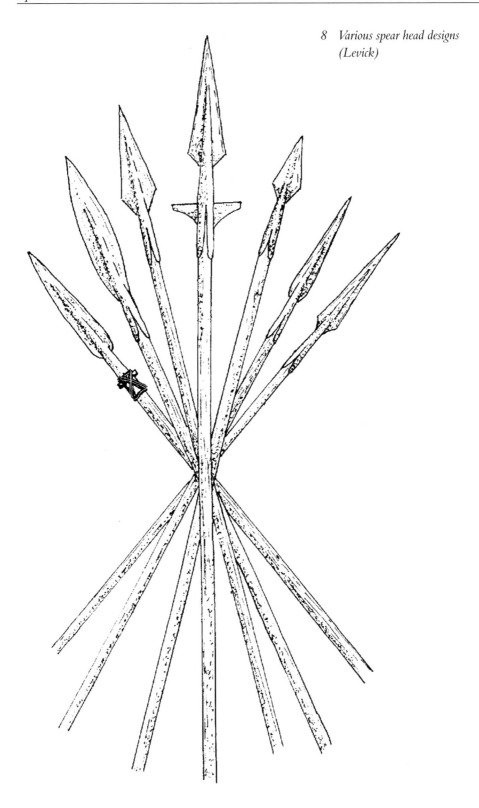

9   Spear blade cross sections

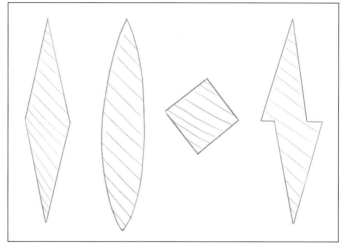

Whether equipped with a flint head by a mammoth hunter or a sophisticated forged triangular point in the hands of a nineteenth-century cavalryman the spear is, and has remained, an excellent weapon for imposing your will on your enemy.

The Vikings and Saxons used them extensively, both in battle and for hunting. In the famous epic poem *The Battle of Maldon*, Eorl Bryhtnoth personally killed two Vikings 'with spear and shield', only then drawing his sword to take on a third. There are four basic designs of spearheads and there was a huge range of heads in use. Angular blades with a diamond cross section make up the great majority of finds, followed by leaf-shaped blades that are normally lenticular in section. Some of the larger examples of these types are so broad in the blade that one is brought to the conclusion that they were used as a slashing weapon in addition to thrusting, much in the manner of the later halberd. Next, a third group are based upon a square- or diamond-shaped bar. These would have been very useful for penetrating mail with or without the addition of a welded-on blade like the spearhead found at Fairford in Gloucestershire. By accident or design, there is a fourth group that has been described as corrugated in section, although the profile of the blade might be either leaf-shaped or angular. These stepped blades are certainly strong in section, but I remain unconvinced that they were intentionally made with that purpose in mind.

Technically, there is little to choose between the heads used for one or the other — unless you are trying to kill pigs. Wild boar have a renowned habit of trying to get to you even though run through with a spear, so spears used for this purpose have stops on the socket, big flanged things like wings. These are supposed to stop the angry creature getting to you and one imagines that they work pretty well. However, not all 'wings' on spears are there for this purpose. Some discovered heads have little flanges no wider than the blade itself and these must have a different purpose. Over the last 20 years I have experimented with winged spears in various ways and have come to the conclusion that they have a specific purpose and are not there just to be different.

The smallest wing can be used to great effect in parrying other spears or swords and are extremely effective at trapping and blocking an opponent's weapon whilst your companion deals with him!

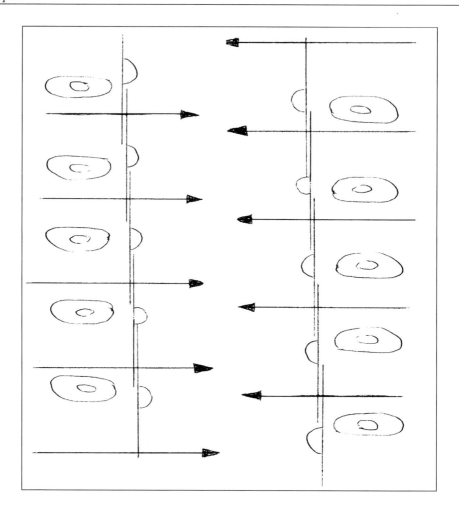

10 Close order shield and spear work, normally called rim-to-boss

With the trailing edge of the wings sharpened, one can have a second chance at damaging the enemy if the spear thrust has been deflected. Obviously, he will be keen to get his shield back in place as quickly as possible but if you keep your spear in contact with the rim as you withdraw it, there might be an opportunity to catch him unawares with a quick ripping stroke, cutting into the muscles of his upper arm or leg. If lucky, the attacker might even be able to hamstring his opponent. Either way, whilst not an immediate knock down blow, it would be very painful and bloody with the real possibility of crippling the enemy so badly as to make him a weak point in the shield wall.

It is also possible to use the wing to pull open a shield by catching at the rim. This is difficult to counter, especially if you are busy attempting to avoid someone else's attempts to kill you. The man on the puller's left thrusts into the gap thus exposed, very often getting in a rib or gut shot at little risk to either party. Working together as a trained unit, two warriors can despatch a number of men quite quickly with this gambit. If the enemy's

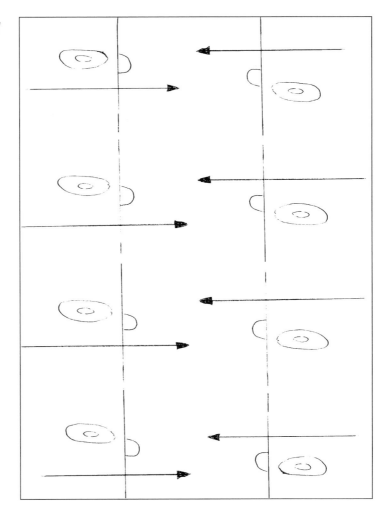

11 *Open order shield
and spear work
(rim-to-rim)*

line is thin, a group of half-a-dozen determined men can easily break the opposition's shield wall or weaken it to the extent that the sensible field commander will attempt to withdraw it in order to regroup.

In this context particularly, spears evolve to a useful length depending on various factors. It is difficult to say with any certainty that a particular spear find was originally this or that length, but common sense dictates that they would have been mainly between 7ft and 9ft (2-3m) long. Any shorter and the principal advantage of keeping your enemy at least a whole pace away from you is gone: any longer and they become unwieldy and too wobbly to use accurately. Thickening up the shaft will make the spear clumsy and heavy and more readily knocked out of the user's hands. The use of spear and shield in warfare throughout history has been inextricably linked, and the interested reader will find more of this aspect of warfare in the chapter on shields.

Entirely aside from the obvious use of being able to kill your enemy beyond the reach of your arm, the spear has the real advantage that it used a minimal amount of expensive

12 *In this manuscript illustration, the stance is correct and it takes a moment to notice that the spear passes behind the head so as not to obscure the face of an important man (Levick)*

iron in its construction. The great majority of spearheads would be made from wrought iron and be small, neat little things with a thick spine to support the cutting edge. There were spearheads of all shapes and sizes, though not in the same numbers. Some were of high-grade steel or sometimes even pattern welded. Others would betray their ancestry as reused broken knives or sword blades. In extremis, it is the work of a few minutes to turn big iron nails into perfectly acceptable spear-heads with a few knowing raps of the smith's hammer.

Two techniques of using a spear are available. One with the spear held high and single-handed as illustrated in the majority of manuscript illustrations. Use of this method allows spearmen to stand close together but demand that they can only fight over-arm in a block. Although well shielded, the wounded (and dead, come to that) cannot be removed and it is very difficult indeed to manoeuvre the unit once formed.

However, allowing the men to take a pace sideways brings the line to open order. Slipping one's arm and shoulder through the shield strap and catching the bottom end of that strap with the left thumb where it is attached to the shield, ensures that no one can readily pull your shield open. It also allows the fingers of the left hand to be used to hold the spear shaft in a loose, sliding grip. The line can now be advanced at the trot if required, although it takes constant nagging to keep it together. The wise commander will bring it to a halt before contact, allowing the slowest to catch up before taking the line into battle at a stepping pace. Serious, determined faces in the line, a couple of older men standing at the back with the standard, a number of loose, quick men with a mixture of long and short weapons looking expectantly around them in order to protect their friends backs and the unit is ready for battle.

So far, we have only looked at the spear as a hand-held close-quarter weapon, but the light throwing spear or javelin was also in common use. Weighing about one or two pounds (0.5-1.0kg) they are light enough to hurl a considerable distance. Experiments show that 40-50 paces is not an unreasonable distance at which to throw one and I have personally witnessed one of our spears hurled over 70 paces by an ex-county standard javelin thrower. Several lines of trained men throwing in succession can have been no fun at all to bear. Each warrior can carry three small spears in their left hand and a fourth in their right hand, so a circulating group of 10 men can deliver 40 sharp and deadly missiles in a steady hail lasting two or three minutes. The lightweight spears will nonetheless penetrate a leather-clad lime wood shield board, pierce riveted mail and wreak death and injury upon a group of men in either close or open order. In practical experiments, we were surprised to find that the spearhead did not need to be razor sharp to deliver a deadly wound. The carcass of a pig could be easily penetrated, a thrown spear passing both into and out of the chest cavity. A mail shirt made some difference, but even then the spearhead cut through it to a depth of 5in (13cm), certainly enough to spoil one's whole day.

The spear can also be used on horseback and a spear thrown from this moving platform is quite devastating. The author has witnessed a spear thrown at the gallop penetrate a wooden shield and the dummy warrior behind it, pinning both to the ground at an angle of 45 degrees. At the end of the Viking Age, the Normans were beginning to use the lance from horseback, against other mounted warriors or against infantry.

The spear was the most commonly-used weapon of the pre-gunpowder period. Used by high and low alike, it was the first line of defence and assault and any re-enactment of the combat of this period must necessarily be based upon its use. Unique amongst the weapons in use at the time, it is cheap to produce in quantity and it takes only about 20 minutes to train a complete novice to use spear and shield sufficiently well to make them more dangerous to their enemies than to their friends. Intensive training and drill — particularly drill — over a period of about six weekends will turn a group of enthusiastic young men and women of no particular ability into a determined and fearsome fighting force.

4 Shield

I am an exile, iron-wounded,
blade-battered, battle-sated,
sword-weary. War I see often,
fight foes. I fear no comfort
or help comes for me in cruel strife
before I am wrecked among warriors,
but hammered blades hack me,
hard-edged hate-sharp handwork of smiths
strikes me in strongholds;
I must stay for a crueller clash.
No cure was ever found by folk in their fields
which could heal my wounds with herbs,
but day and night through deadly blows
the swords' wounds widen in my flesh.

Anglo-Saxon riddle

The large circular shield of the Vikings was part of a conservative tradition of manufacture. The only intact examples from the Viking Age founding the Scandinavian homeland are those that lined the gunwales of the buried warship from Gokstad, Norway (**13**) dated to *c.*AD 905. They are similar to shields from Thorsberg bog and other Danish weapon deposits of the Roman Iron Age, 500-700 years previously. Though archaeological evidence dries up with the adoption of Christian burial rites, art sources (such as the Lewis chessmen) indicate that kite shields were accepted in the Norse lands in the twelfth century, along with small round bucklers, an example of which is kept in the Oslo collection.

Construction and dimensions

Shields were typically 2ft 7in-3ft (80-90cm) in diameter (Table 1). The board was flat, and made of a single layer of planks butted together. Softwood from conifers seems to have been used in most, but not all cases. The Gokstad shields were made of seven or eight white pine planks of varying widths, and only $\frac{1}{4}$in (7mm) thickness — their uniformity and fragile design might suggest that they were not combat shields but ornaments made especially for the burial, however a multitude of other finds indicate that planks were in fact normally only $\frac{1}{4}$in-$\frac{5}{16}$in (6-10mm) thick (Table 2), and could be bevelled even thinner at the outer edge.

Although at least some shields from Birka had a thin leather facing, and some earlier English shields were covered on both sides, the planks of the Gokstad shields were painted, indicating that they had no leather covering them. An interesting parallel to the Gokstad shields comes from a peat bog at Tirskom, in Latvia. Dated to the ninth century, this near-intact shield is constructed of six spruce or fir planks covered on front and rear with leather, which was padded with pressed grass. Planks were possibly glued edge-to-edge, extra support would come from the leather covering, as well as fastenings for the boss, grip and rim bindings (see below). There is no archaeological evidence for laminated (i.e. cross-ply) construction, though contemporary German poetry and slightly later Norwegian legislation suggest it.

Table 1. Estimated diameters of Viking age shields from archaeological finds in Northern Europe. All are dated to the tenth century, except the Tirskom shield (ninth century) and the Krimylda shield (eleventh century). For comparison, here are the dimensions of a number of pre-Viking shields: from pagan Anglo-Saxon graves (23 examples) 1ft 4in to 3ft (42-92cm) diameter; Thorsberg moor find, Denmark (seven examples, Roman Iron Age) 2ft 1in to 3ft 5in (65-104cm) diameter; Valsgarde, Sweden (3 examples, Vendel period) 2ft 9in to 3ft 7in (84-110cm) diameter

SITE	Diameter (cm)	Method of determination
Ballateare, Man	?~75	decayed remains of wood
Birka, Sweden		
Bj 628	95	surviving metal rim
Bj 736	80	surviving metal rim
Bj 842	?90	surviving metal rim
Bj 886	>70	length of intact grip
Bj 1098	>90	width of grave
Gokstad, Norway	94	intact shield
Grimstrup, Denmark	~95	decayed remains of wood*
Krimylda, Latvia	80	decayed remains of wood*
Rends, Denmark		length of fragmentary grip
Tirskom, Latvia (1)		intact shield
(2)	~73	remains of one plank

* this object is a circular board which cannot definitely be identified as a shield (no boss or other traces)

Table 2. Thicknesses of Viking-Age shields from archaeological finds. Most of these graves are probably tenth-century, except Tirskom (ninth-century). For comparison, shields from (much earlier) pagan Anglo-Saxon graves average 0.75cm thick (103 examples, data from Dickinson and Herke)

NATIONALITY Site & Grave no.	Thickness of wood (cm)	Part of shield	Method* of determination	Leather facing?
DENMARK				
Lindholm Høye 1112	0.5-0.6	board edge	C	
NORWAY				
Gokstad	0.7	board	E	
N Myklebost mound 3	~0.5	board		A
	33.0	board & grip	A	
SWEDEN				
Birka:				
Bj 369A	20.4	board edge	C	
Bj 581	0.5-0.6	board	A	
Bj 644	31.6	board & grip	B	
Bj 725	3.5	board & grip	A	
Bj 727	2.1	board & grip	B	Y
Bj 750	31.8	board & grip	B	
Bj 850	0.4	board edge	C	Y (both)
Bj 944	<0.6	board edge	C	
Bj 977	32.8	board & grip	A	
Rothagen	0.5	board	A	
	2.8	board & grip	A	
Ulfsta	31.4	board (& grip?)	D	
Valsgarde 1	20.6	board	A	
	24.0	board & grip	A	
Valsgarde 12	20.6	board edge	C	
MAN				
Cronk Moar	1.0, 1.0	board	A, B	N
32.6,	2.2	board & grip	B, B	
FRANCE				
Ile de Groix	1.3	board	A	
LATVIA				
Tirskom peatbog (1)	0.6	board	E	Y (both)
(2)	1.4	board	E	

★ Estimated thickness measured from: A = clench nails on boss; B = eyelet or nail not passing through boss; C = inside width of edge clamp; D = nail fastening three-lobed grip terminal; E = preserved wooden parts

Table 3. Metal clamps from shield rims: numbers, dimensions, distribution on shield rim (if known)

SITE	No. of clamps	Type and arrangement	Grave*	Dimensions (cm) length	breadth	I.W.**	No. of rivets	Metal
BIRKA								
Bj	451			2.4	2.4			bronze
Bj	369A6	B		2.2-2.5	1.9-2.1	0.4/0.9	2	iron
Bj	5737-10		((	?	?			iron
Bj	581?4		(	?	?	?		iron
Bj	6241-2			?	?	?		iron
Bj	62825-26		o	2.5-2.6	3.0-3.5			tinned iron
Bj	6432	B		2.7	2.0			tinned iron
Bj	736~25	B	o	3.0?	4.5?			iron
Bj	842~45	X		2.6	2.1		2	iron
Bj	8503	B	(	2.0	2.3-2.6	0.5/0.8	?3	bronze
Bj	9141	B		2.5	1.5		2	iron
Bj	9441	A		2.9	2.0	0.6	2	bronze
VALSGARDE								
1219		B	X	3.0-3.5	2.3-2.5	0.6/1.0	2	iron
LINDHOLM HOYE								
11121		B		2.6	3.1	0.5/0.8	3	iron
SCAR(Orkney)								
(boat)?1				?	?			tinned bronze

*   Distribution on shield: o = probable continuous rim; X = evenly spaced but not continuous; (= clustered on one, or ((more part(s) of rim, but not continuous

** I.W. = internal width (i.e. thickness of enclosed wood and leather layers). Measured at opening, as well as maximum width for Type B clamps

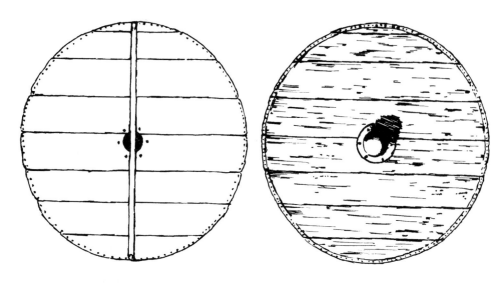

13 A reconstruction of a shield from the Gokstad ship. Lightly constructed and lacking detail fittings, facing and a decent grip, it appears to have not been designed for use but for show or (possibly) a means of temporarily giving the vessel more freeboard

Boss

At the centre of the shield was a circular opening (though oval, 'figure-8', and 'D'-shaped openings are also known from pre-Viking material), covered by a more-or-less hemispherical iron boss of 6in (15cm) diameter (including flange), which enclosed the handgrip. The iron at the apex of the dome was fairly thick $\frac{3}{16}$ in (3-5mm), though the flange was somewhat thinner, demonstrating that bosses were not dished out of a flat sheet of metal — rather, the dome was forged directly from a billet of iron, then the flange was beaten out from the edge.

Bosses had two main forms and some variants (**14**). The early style had a high dome and a pronounced neck type Rygh (R564). The main later style, low domed without a neck (R562), never completely replaced the former. Less common was a squat style (R563) and a sub-conical style (R565), sometimes with an apical knob (not illustrated). The Balnekiel find in northern Scotland has a heavy boss that is basically domed in cross section but also has a neck. It is difficult to see why this was done and proved extremely difficult to replicate.

The boss was normally attached by broad-headed iron nails, the points of which were either clenched (bent over) or flattened on the reverse of the shield. In the Birka material four was the most common number of nails, occasionally six (as for the Gokstad shields). Five nails were also sometimes used, as in examples from Cronk Moar, Man and the Ile de Groix, France. The flange of some bosses were angled, perhaps to secure the boss to the board by placing tension on the nails, or possibly because they were attached to convex shield boards.

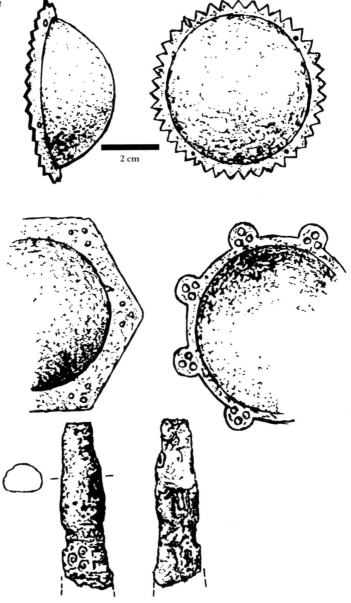

14 *Shield boss designs. In the Viking Age, most were simple dome-shaped constructions raised from a flat iron sheet by hammering. Flanges varied occasionally like this example that was decorated with small nails*

2 cm

Embellishment, if present, was simple. Flanges with decorative edgings of non-ferrous metal strips were found in some Birka graves (**15**), and nail heads were sometimes inlaid or tinned. Single examples of bosses with a toothed flange are known from Telemark, Norway (**15 top**); Birka, Sweden; and Ilede Groix, France. In the latter burial, a cremation with a large ship, several bosses with elaborate flanges of unparalleled design were found (**14**). These bosses may have had a Western European origin.

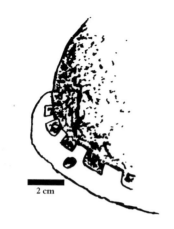

2 cm

15 *Decorated shield bosses. Top, boss with toothed flange from Telemark, Norway. Centre, from Birka (Bj544) showing sheet tin applique on flange. Bottom, side view (Bj581) showing nails clenched over for retention*

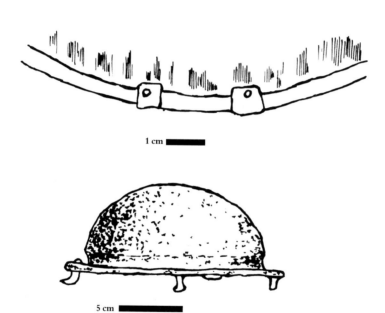

1 cm

5 cm

Handle or grip

Wood alone must have been used in the majority of graves where remains are lacking, as in the Gokstad shields where a thin lath of rectangular section is nailed, crossways with respect to the planks, from edge to edge across the back face, it serves as a handle where it crosses the central hole (**18, 19**). On more elaborate shields a spindle-shaped wooden core was covered by a gutter-shaped sheathing of iron, usually ornamented with embossed bronze sheet or silver inlay (**16**).

The handle was long, often crossing the full diameter of the shield, and was tapered towards both ends. The sheath could be flattened out into a spatulate terminal which

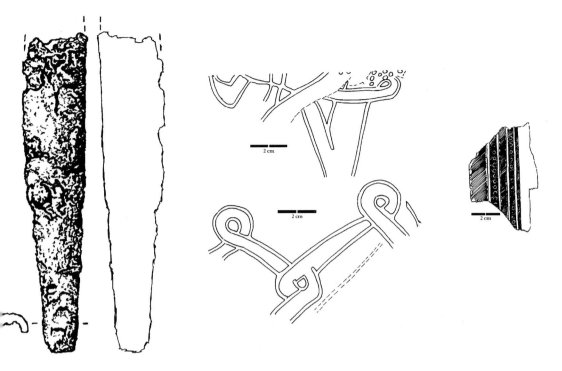

16 *Shield fittings.*
   Left: fragment of silver-embellished iron grip with wooden core from Hedeby ship grave at
   Schleswig-Holstein, Germany.
   Right; fragment of decorated gesso covering from the Ballateare find in the Isle of Man

was nailed directly to the board (**19**), or be fastened down by separate bronze mounts (**17**). Occasionally a pair of extra-long nails was used in fastening the boss, which shows that they also passed through the handle (see Table 2 for examples). The handgrip may have been wrapped with leather (e.g. Birka grave Bj504, and as known from early Anglo-Saxon finds).

Judging by material from Man, the Hebrides and Ireland, some Scandinavian settlers in the Irish Sea region adopted a less robust shield design, with a small conical boss and a solid metal grip with disc terminals, probably typical of native Celtic weaponry.

Edge reinforcement

Continuous gutter-shaped metal edge bindings like those known from Vendel, Valsgarde, and Thorsbjerg were obsolete by the Viking Age. In the vast majority of finds there is no evidence of edge reinforcement, which must therefore have been absent, or of a perishable nature. On the Gokstad shields, small holes are bored about 1in (2cm) in from the edge,

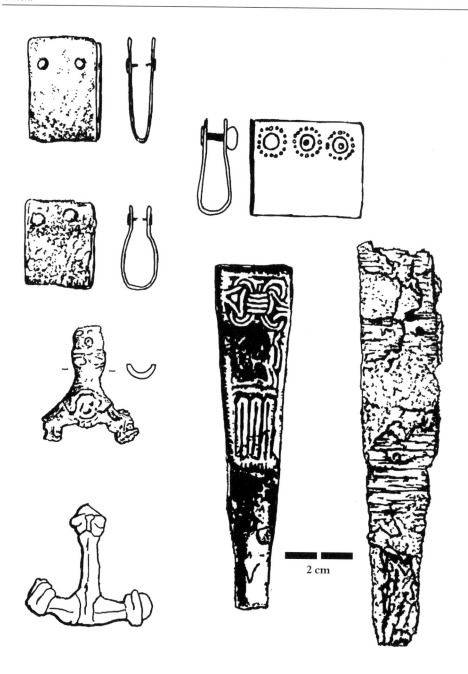

17 *Various shield fittings. Top left, simple rim clamp. Right, decorating around the rivet heads. Below, left, clamp to secure leather edging. Two images, bottom left, decorative fittings. Bottom right, two grip extensions in decorated metal*

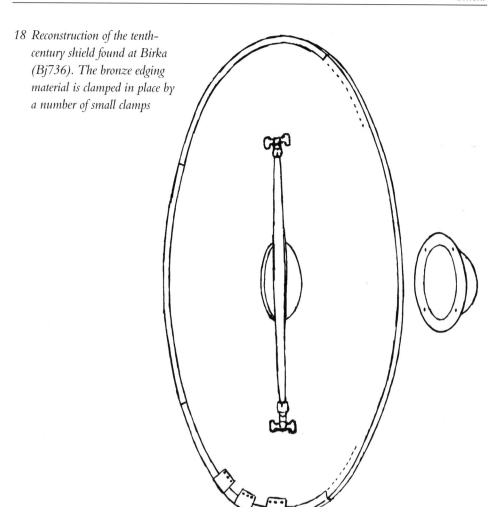

18 Reconstruction of the tenth-century shield found at Birka (Bj736). The bronze edging material is clamped in place by a number of small clamps

at intervals of $1\frac{1}{4}$in (3.5cm) (**13 & 18**), presumably to fasten a rim, all other traces of which have perished. It can be speculated that the edge was bound with a leather strip fastened with stitches or thongs, or possibly very fine iron nails.

Small clamps made of iron or bronze sheet are occasionally found in graves (Table 3; **17**). Sometimes several clamps are distributed evenly around the shield rim, perhaps to fasten a leather edge binding, traces of which sometimes remain. Clamps from Birka grave Bj 850 were fastened over a leather edging (**18**), though their low number and uneven distribution suggests that this was not their primary purpose. Here they might have fastened joins between planks, or shored up a damaged edge. In Birka graves Bj 628 and 736 the clamps were butted to produce a continuous edge (**19**), however, only sections of the rim survive, perhaps indicating deliberate damage before burial. Clamps were sometimes simply decorated by tinning, punching or engraving (**17**).

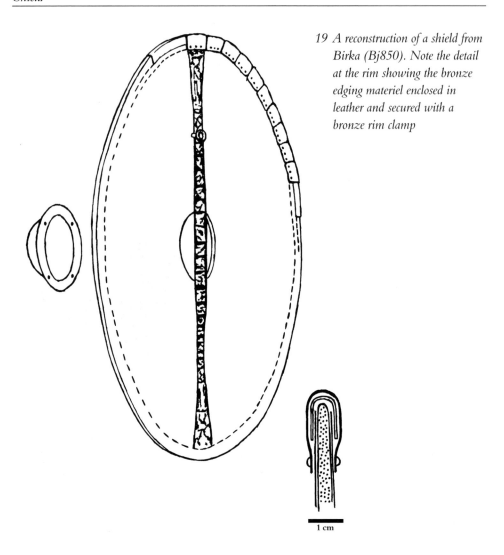

19 *A reconstruction of a shield from Birka (Bj850). Note the detail at the rim showing the bronze edging materiel enclosed in leather and secured with a bronze rim clamp*

1 cm

Other fixtures

Other metal fittings from shields, including nails, are occasionally recovered. Some Birka graves contained one or two small rings held by eyelets (**17**) that passed through the boards, and sometimes also the handle, with the ring projecting on the rear side. They may have served to hang up the shield, or as attachment points for a shoulder strap.

In the eleventh-century ValsgSrde 11 burial, a shield appears to have been repaired by nailing 13 thin brass strips across the break.

20   *Shields in art. Horsemen on Gotland picture stones. Silver shield pendent from Birka,*
     Sweden. Bronze Valkeri pendant. Tapestry fragments. Thor's hammer. Two shield-like
     pendants. Ring and staple fitting, possibly for strap attachment (Birka)

Decoration

Archaeology as well as literary and art sources indicate that the shield was often painted.
The faces of the Gokstad shields were painted yellow (?orpiment = arsenous trioxide) or
black (?charcoal), and arranged alternately along the ship's sides. Red shields may have
been popular. A red shield is mentioned on a Danish runestone, as well as in several sagas.

51

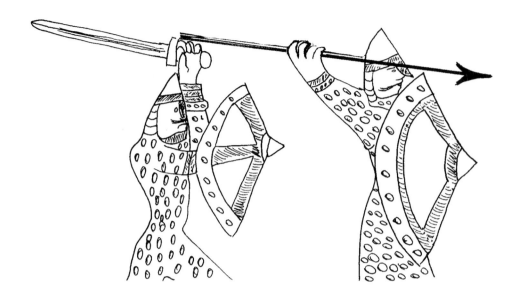

21 The different stance of the shield-bearing warrior when using sword or spear is demonstrated here in this drawing of two saxon huscarls on the Bayeux Tapestry

Distribution of a pigment layer in the Viking Age Valsgarde 9 grave indicated a red painted shield. Shields from the Roman Iron Age weapon sacrifice at Thorsberg were painted red or blue. Red pigments in ancient paints seem to derive from mineral sources i.e. red ochre (haematite, ferric oxide — as on a figurine from the Danish royal mounds at Jelling); or cinnabar (mercuric sulphide, as on the Illerup shield of *c*.AD 200: Forhistoriskmuseet, Moesgard Denmark). Also on the Jelling figurine was a dark blue paint made by mixing powdered white chalk with burnt organic matter (charcoal?), and a yellow of orpiment in an oil base.

Fragments from Ballateare, Man suggest that the leather facing of this shield was painted with black and red patterns on a white background — it has been suggested that *gesso* (ground chalk in an organic matrix, like egg white) had been used to prepare the surface. Traces of white paint were also found on a wooden fragment from the Manx Cronk Moar shield.

A recently discovered tenth-century chamber grave at Grimstrup, Denmark (Esbjerg Museum) contained a circular wooden board that covered the corpse from head to hip. As no other usual traces (i.e. boss) were found in an otherwise fully equipped male burial, it has been suggested that the board is a 'blank' or unfinished shield. The board was elaborately painted with interlace patterns, although the overall design is no longer discernible. The background colour is dark blue, the interlace is grey-green edged with white lines. Some lines of red paint and white dots are also visible.

Representations of shields in Viking art are frequently marked with 'pinwheel' patterns of radiating curved lines. These might possibly represent metal strengthening bands, unknown from archaeology but required in later law codes for levy equipment; or even

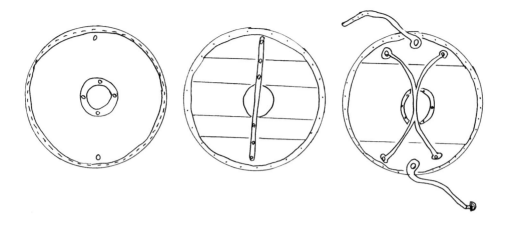

22 Shields back and front rim may be rawhide leather or iron

seams in the leather facing; or may mark segments originally painted in contrasting colours, as shown in a few contemporary Frankish manuscripts. Inspiration for decoration of a reconstructed shield might also be sought in surviving painted wooden objects from the Viking Age.

Sheet metal decorations in the form of beasts or birds fixed to the shield face are confined to the preceding Vendel period, though an appliqué of wooden strips was suggested for the Cronk Moar shield. Some examples of decorated metal parts (bosses, grips, clamps) from Viking Age shields have already been mentioned above.

Combat techniques

Analysis of possible battle-type damage to weapons from the massive deposit of Nydham indicated that the blows that so damaged the weapons were inflicted deliberately. Research shows that a sword (for instance) was held point downwards and the cuts into the metal are directed from the hilt end of the weapon, not the point. Whilst not conclusive, this was probably done to 'kill' the weapon, so that it could not be used in the afterworld. The heavy iron construction of the Viking Age boss is, however, unlike the Nydham examples of thin bronze, perhaps indicating changes in the hand-to-hand fighting style to one in which parries with the boss were expected. The use of shields in close combat is well attested in the sagas, notably in the *holmgang* duel. The custom of allowing replacement shields to be used in *holmgangs* underlines their fragility. Although the thin boards would split easily, they could have been deliberately made in order to snare an attacker's blade, and so perhaps pull them off-balance while delivering a counterstroke.

In open-field combat, shields were usually used to form a shield-wall, sometimes referred to as a burgh. For maximum protection, the warriors turn side on to their enemy and scrunch up tight behind their shields, each one overlapping his neighbour's shield by half the width of the shield. In re-enactment, this is called 'rim-to-boss'. It leaves precious little room for manoeuvre but does have the advantage of great strength and a number of determined, trained, disciplined men advancing together a pace at a time in this way is very difficult to stop. Most men will be using the ubiquitous spear in their right hands and this weapon will be used single-handed and from above shoulder height in a stabbing motion. Spear length varies in the archaeological record, but a good average is around 8-9ft (about 2.5m). Second and third rows of warriors can easily be accommodated in this formation, although their shields are of little use to them pressed up against the backs of their friends in the rank in front. Experiments indicate that it makes more sense for rearward ranks to stand back a little, ready to cover the formation against missiles in a loose kind of testudo. They would then be in an excellent position to retreat, move sideways or press forward to resist a concentrated attack like a pig-snout.

In the *Carmen de Hastingae Prolio*, it says of the Saxon shield wall at Hastings that the wall became so tight towards the end of the battle that the dead could not fall. Indeed, the author has been in similar positions on occasion when a discarded spear did not fall to the ground when dropped and a sword had to be drawn a foot at a time until it was clear of the scabbard! This kind of situation results in great loss of life and it is difficult to survive when an attack is pressed home in such a way.

If the shield wall breaks up, then the individual spearman finds himself in a much more dangerous position. Usually, the warrior will revert to the slung shield position and use the spear two handed whilst still avoiding the risk that an enemy can bash open his shield like a door. A spear is only an advantage when your enemy is beyond the sharp end and any swordsman worth his salt should be able to strike the stabbing spear away from the bodyline and press home his attack with speed. There are techniques whereby the defensive spearman can literally throw the weapon back through his hands to maintain the sharp point in the killing zone, but a better bet is to keep a short knife in the right hand whilst controlling the spear with the same hand. It sounds complicated, but in fact it works well.

Using a short weapon, most warriors out of a shield wall will prefer to use the shield by its central grip, catching the shoulder strap up in their left hands to avoid having a loop of strong leather strap hanging invitingly below the shield's rim in the six o'clock position. Thus equipped, the shield becomes much more active and is used as a weapon as well as a means of defence, enabling the user to punch with the boss and perhaps use the rim to pull open the shield of an unsuspecting enemy. Two Saxon warriors from the Bayeux Tapestry exhibit just this point in **21**.

Although one would avoid sinking a spear point into a shield or cutting down with a sword into the end grain of unprotected wooden planks, it is unavoidable in the long run and fierce tugging matches ensue. These are to the advantage of neither party and one or the other — or frequently both — will be killed by enemies either side of them in the shield wall or by passers by in open field combats. As a general rule, if the weapon doesn't come free with the second pull, one is well advised to let go of it when your enemy pulls again. This leaves him with a weapon stuck in his shield, making it unwieldy in the extreme. The sensible man will have equipped himself with a secondary weapon and he can swiftly despatch his encumbered foe and retrieve his weapon at his leisure. It is

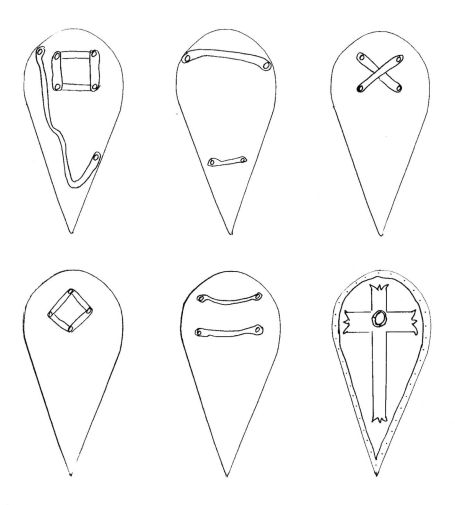

23 Various forms of strapping on kite shield backs. Reconstructed from images on the Bayeux Tapestry. Bottom right shows a typical facing

possible that the short axe so popular with the Viking warrior was used principally for destroying shields to soften up the shield wall to missile attack.

Plain shields of pine planks simply will not take this kind of abuse and are quickly destroyed, perhaps within minutes of the battle starting. It is hard to see how any warrior would willingly have gone into battle thus equipped and it is quite possible that excavated shields that are not covered in leather or cloth were never intended for use in a battlefield context. After all, it is the symbolism of the shield as a means of protection that was important in a burial. The Gokstad find is another example of this and here the shield was simply used for display or as a means of temporarily raising the freeboard of the ship at sea.

The evolution of spear-and-shield combat in the late twentieth century

At the end of the day, it is training that makes the difference. A well-trained and disciplined force of men that is responsive to orders and has a good *esprit du corps* will always win against a rabble of ill-trained individuals, each one out for their own glory. And that's what the Vikings had, trained and hardened warriors who had sailed and fought and lived together.

When I first started in military recreation in 1980 at the ripe old age of 38, everyone in Dark Age re-enactment fought with strapped arm shields and single-handed broadswords. Spears were actively discouraged as they were seen as a dangerous weapon — more of which anon. It was true that no-one wore horns on their helmets anymore, but there were one or two helmets about that still had their sockets, which gives some idea of the state of play.

The group I ran in Bristol — always known simply as 'Wessex' (but often prefixed with one coarse expletive or another!) — were then at the cutting edge of re-enactment innovation and were the first to produce purpose-made shield bosses and spearheads in the autumn of 1984. At first, the spearheads were sharp and we only flung them at targets. However, it was not long before it occurred to me that a ball-ended spear would be safe to fight with. As an efficient way of dispatching the enemy it proved to have no peer, particularly when used with a shield that was slung from the shoulder by its cross-strap.

During the next season, we went through a period of rapid evolution. The shield wall was still basically shield and sword, but the shield was becoming much more manoeuvrable as we changed over from strapped arm to centre gripped and bossed construction. During this time spearheads were still rare and we only had about seven or eight spread amongst a group of 35 or so combatants. The heads were big and heavy and the shafts were thick and strong, but used from behind the shield wall, they were utterly devastating. Whilst we obviously took losses, it became quite rare for Wessex to be on the losing side. Despite all the evidence to the contrary, our opponents still clung to their sword-based combat technique which had been the norm for six or seven years — two generations on re-enactment terms.

The following winter, Wessex went all out to equip our line with spears that were light enough to be used single-handed and evolved a lightweight and reliable spearhead. We started to have them made in bulk and selling on at cost-price, a definite aid to equipping our little army as it should be according to the available evidence.

We saw that it was now very important to stay together and great efforts were made in maintaining the integrity of the shield wall. We practised weekly and actually invented a form of drill — complete with Old Norse or Anglo-Saxon commands — which we instilled into our warriors from the first day they took up weapons. It proved a great success and the Wessex shield wall became extremely efficient and swept all before it, frequently 'killing' the enemy in a few minutes despite being heavily outnumbered and doing it without the loss of a single man.

We became arrogant and — I have no doubt — somewhat overbearing (who ever heard of a humble successful warrior). Every year we expected more spears to appear in the shield walls of our enemies, but, by and large, this never happened although there were some exceptions. In the end, the ruling clique did the obvious thing and flung us all out into the darkness, there to wither and die. So we formed Regia Anglorum instead.

As Regia Anglorum grew, we formed our own enemy, now all carrying spears, and Wessex encountered some real opposition. We had established 7ft (2.13m) spears as a norm, but 9ft (2.70m) were available to the more experienced warrior.

We quickly found that each warrior has three enemies: the one in front of him and the one on his shielded side, neither of whom were likely to kill the experienced man. His real enemy was the man on his right who can see through the narrow diagonal gap left between the shield rim should the shield wall fail and the line break, even for a moment. I have personally seen a line collapse in three or four seconds as the man in the centre makes a mistake and the first kill is rapidly followed up by skilled fighters.

Using 9ft (2.70m) spears, the man in the line has five enemies, because two more can now reach him. Typically, you never see who kills you.

Almost all the round shields one sees in reconstructions of early medieval combat are flat in cross section and as far as I have been able to ascertain, no found example appears to be constructed of anything other than flat boards. It is possible to make a case for flat boards being thinned towards the edge on one side, thus giving a slightly curved face — but I am not convinced. However, there is excellent pictorial evidence on the Bayeux Tapestry that lenticular rounds were in use: in fact, every representation of a round shield shows it in cross section as if to make the point clearly. Perhaps they were a new idea, we shall probably never know.

Whilst a lenticular round shield does wrap around you and give somewhat better protection if is held close to the body, flat boards do have advantages. Deflected weapons do not skid off into your face so readily and it is a lot easier to make a really tight shield wall with flats.

The armies at this time used a form of attack called the pig-snout or swine-array. The easiest way to imagine it is as a pyramid of men, one at the front, two behind him, five behind them and so on. Their shield will be carried overhead by the men in the middle and to the left on the left-hand side of the unit. It is tempting to allow the men on the right to use their shields in the 'wrong' hand, but as the block moves quickly it is probably unnecessary. At the back is a separate open line of good men who protect the backs of their friends during the attack. The man at the point of the pyramid must be big, strong, sturdily made and well equipped with padding and armour. Interestingly, he does not run with the rest, but actually leans backward, resisting the onrush as well as he can. This ensures that the formation stays tightly packed as it relies upon its density for penetration.

The impact pressure is tremendous, I have known small people trampled underfoot, arms sprained, shoulders dislocated and many a bloody lip from the crash of shields. In one well-remembered incident, the man at the front was a big, burly man of around 18 stone called Stewart (as he was such a big Stew, we called him Casserole) and the target was the sally port door of a palisade we'd built for an event. The impact pressure was so great that the door was wrenched out of the hole, hinges, door jamb and all. Cass was jammed in the woodwork somehow, contriving to be thrust into a 9in gap from which he had to be extricated with a crowbar and no little damage to the structure. It was hard for the men to work as they were laughing so much. After the battle and divested of his war gear, it proved impossible to get him back into the narrow space.

But all this effort is useless without a sense of timing. Without support, the pig-snout will probably be allowed to penetrate the shield wall, a number of warriors detailed to cut them off and deal with them as they are vulnerable in a block. I have commanded flying blocks that drove a hole in the opposition's shield wall and kept going in a circle to charge as a block into the back of the enemy line, much to their considerable consternation. I have seen others that simply kept going at full speed, their job done, returning to their own side without the loss of a man.

As a field commander, mounting a charge like this can lose you a dozen or so of your best men if they are not supported. After the pig-snout sets off, the sensible commander will set his whole shield wall in motion at the charge no more than two seconds later. The timing is critical, as the bulk of the warriors must arrive in time to take maximum advantage of the disruption their friends have caused. A fragmented shield wall in good training can reform with lightning speed and your men must be there in time to despatch the flattened, engage the wary and frighten the unwilling.

If you have enough men, a second wave of lightly-equipped combatants should arrive about ten seconds after the main wall to engage the flanks and rear. They run forward together in loose order, shouting their heads off, splitting into two units as they get close to the struggling mass of men in the middle of the field. Arriving at the flanks, they peel off into open order lines and attack the back of the enemy's line. Timed correctly, this three pronged attack can bring a battle to an end in a few minutes. Brilliant fun for the warriors, but the client may not be so amused having paid for an hour-long show. Never mind, you can raise the dead and do it all over again — that's re-enactment!

Finally, a word about kite shields. Originally developed to protect the left side of a horseman in combat, they appear to have been slowly becoming more common in Northern Europe in the 20 years or so preceding the Battle of Hastings. The great majority of the shields shown on the Bayeux Tapestry are kites. Although trends move somewhat slower in the Viking homelands, it is reasonable to assume that this form of defence was reaching there too. I would be amazed if Hardrada did not have one at Stamford Bridge in September 1066.

The Tapestry goes to some lengths to show us that the kites it illustrates were not gripped in the same way as a round shield, despite the fact that kites appear to be bossed as well as rounds. Most can be seen to be gripped by a more or less horizontal strap across the widest part of the shield. Other sources indicate a square of leather straps that can be held in a number of different ways. From below, with the arm thrust through the lower strap and gripping the upper or from the left with the arm slid under the first vertical and gripping the second vertical strap. One can sling it from the neck by a separate cross strap, or, with the addition of a further strap fitted two thirds of the way down, run the arm through one of the upper straps and grip the lowest. This latter arrangement can be seen in use on the Tapestry and it allows one to use the point of the kite offensively.

5 Armour

Bright were their byrnies, hard and hand-linked;
In their shining armour the ring mail sang

Beowulf

The drenched acre of earth first fathered me out of its frozen womb.
My mind knows I was not knit from woollen fleece or twined from hair.
No weft was woven in me, no warp I have, no throngs of thread sang my tissue,
no whirring shuttle snaked my flesh nor loom-bar laced me with its blows.
Worms' weird skill did not weave me, spinning beauty in their golden webs.
Yet all over earth I am honoured, held in heroes' high esteem.
Thought-skilled men, thoroughly wise in words, will guess this garment's name.

Anglo-Saxon riddle

Every warrior would have done what he could to protect his soft body from the impact of weapons. The human body is singularly ill-equipped to deal with wounding, lacking thickness of skin or density of fur. But it is our species alone that has developed single pair disputes over breeding partners or hunting territory into tribal warfare of a level of sophistication where considerable areas of the planet may be laid waste. Going into battle requires protection and every warrior society on earth has made what arrangements they could to provide for their combatants.

Body protection in use in the Viking Age consisted of padded cloth and leather and mail. There was no plate and there is precious little evidence for scale and none at all for lameller. Although scale armour was in fairly frequent use by Roman troops, there

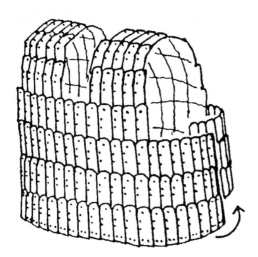

24 Scale armour. Note the overlap is upwards (Nicoloson)

is virtually no evidence for its continued use. A very thin case can be made for the use of scale by returning members of the Varangian Guard from Constantinople, but there are no finds to support its use in the north, and home-grown examples must have been rare indeed.

Padded armour used by the Romans of the Late Empire was called *thoracomachus* or *subarmalis* and was certainly in use by the legions in the late fourth and early fifth century. Anyone who has ever worn a mail shirt in battle re-enactment (let alone the real thing!) will know that a padded jack (1) relieves the weight of the mail by spreading it across a larger area of the body; (2) that it absorbs the weight of blows; and (3) is a great comfort on a cold day. In addition, it forms a good basis for a makeshift bed, separating the body from the chilling ground.

The mail may turn the edge of the blade, but without padding below the mail it will transmit the shock onward without spreading it much, thus shattering bone and tearing sinew. There is almost nothing of this padding in the archaeological record as linen, wool and perhaps leather leaves little trace in the ground. The Visby mass grave yields examples, but caution leads me to say that there are no secure finds or indisputable tertiary evidence. Manuscript evidence by way of the written word and drawings are notoriously open to interpretation — for instance, William the Conqueror's brother Bishop Odo appears to be wearing an exceptional piece of kit on the Bayeux Tapestry as it bears a striking resemblance to 1970s kitchen lino (**colour plate 7**). I once saw a faithful reproduction of the Tapestry's image created out of triangles of different coloured leathers, painstakingly sewn together into body armour. Unfortunately, it was heavy, intractable and (to our modern eyes) amusing to observe in use and as far as I know it only ever had the one outing.

My experience indicates that to wear mail without padded protection is plain foolishness. In general, this form of armour follows the lines of a mail shirt worn above it and would probably have consisted of tubes, squares or diamond-shaped cells sewn into a multi-layered garment of coarse linen or leather. These cells are stuffed with scrap cloth,

25 A close-up of modern welded mail

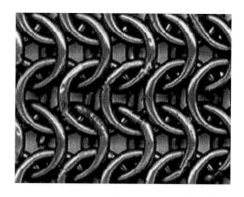

raw fleece or horsehair and sewn shut row by row. When finished, a well-made padded jack will stand up unaided. By the end of the eleventh century, scale and lamellae armour were in use in the Middle East and those knights who had been on Crusade to the Holy Land might well have brought some back with them.

It is a common mistake to use the term 'chain mail', a term that did not come into use until the middle years of the eighteenth century. The root of the word mail is from the Latin *macula*, meaning dots or spots or mesh and there is a certain logic to this when viewing someone wearing a mail shirt. Even so, until the thirteenth century, there is no evidence for this form of body protection being called mail. The Vikings called them 'byrnies' unless they referred to them by a kenning or poetically descriptive phrase like 'the net of the spears', 'war-net', 'Odin's web'. It will, however, save a lot of confusion if I continue to use the word 'mail' in this context. The mail coat was as much an indication of the professional warrior as the sword and it was always expensive and labour-intensive to produce.

Mail of the period was made by cutting thin strips of iron from a hammered sheet and forging it into a thin rod, one end being thinner than the other. This would then have been heated to cherry red and swiftly drawn through the first in a series of punched holes in an iron block called a draw-plate. Re-heating and drawing repeatedly through a series of holes of decreasing size forces the wire into an approximately rounded profile. It also does wonders for the grain flow in the iron, making the material stronger than if it had not been hot drawn. The next task is to wind the wire around a rod and, using a sharp chisel, cut the wire into rings. The rings are then driven through a conical hole in another iron block that would make the ends overlap. Half of them are set aside and the rest are flattened at their ends with a small hammer and punch and a second punch is used to drive a hole through the soft iron. The natural wearing of the iron drawing block, the winding and handling will tend to flatten their original sub-circular profile and none I have seen could properly be described as round in section. The other half of the rings are heated at their ends and forged together in a hammer welded joint to make a solid ring. It is easy to say it, but attempts to replicate this process when researching the Anglian helmet found at Coppergate in York found that the smith had just about a second to hit the ring after it left the fire, after that it was too cold to weld.

An alternative method would be to punch flat washers out of an iron sheet, but the technology of the time was incapable of producing a pair of punches in a hard enough

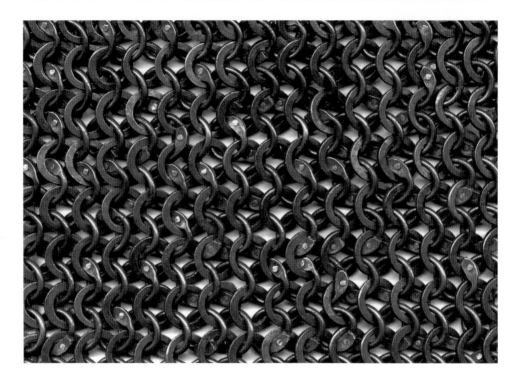

26 A piece of well-made modern riveted mail by Tony Whiticker

material that could repeatedly punch holes in iron without damage or rapid blunting.

Oakshott in his *Dark Age Warrior* refers to a group of Pathan tribesmen who were still making riveted mail into the 1920s. He describes a group of men and boys working on a production line principal, each one involved in one process: drawing, winding, cutting, etc.

As the mail was assembled, a punched ring was linked to four of the welded rings, a tiny rivet being driven through the holes to close the link. Alternatively, the whole shirt could have been made entirely from riveted rings. Wrought iron rusts very slowly, so rust proofing would not have been necessary, although the prudent warrior would keep his byrnie away from seawater.

Although mail in the Viking age was made from soft, wrought iron wire that was always riveted and/or welded shut, experiments today in reconstructive techniques invariably centre around butted mail. The construction is quite inaccurate, butt-linked mail not being in use a thousand years ago. Some is made in mild steel fencing wire in a perfect rounded section and others are made from $\frac{5}{16}$ in (8mm) flat $\frac{1}{16}$ in (1mm) square section spring washers. It must be said that neither style of wire shape is completely accurate, the fencing wire being too round and the washers too flat — and all of them are too even. Within this last year (1999-2000), a specially made flat washer has become commercially available that exactly replicates the $\frac{5}{16}$ in (8mm) 'industry standard' spring washer that is used throughout re-enactment of the early medieval period. These washers have a sharply flat face and the other is slightly rounded, giving a better appearance to the mail when made up. Most mail shirts in re-enactment are made of steel, not iron and this rusts much more quickly than in the original. Therefore, although wholly inaccurate, most modern mail is zinc plated.

As I write at the end of the year 2000, riveted mail is becoming slowly available from India and Mexico, but the quality leaves much to be desired and the price does not reflect this.

It is often forgotten that even though it takes a huge investment of time and effort to make a mail shirt, there were a lot of people doing it and production never stopped, going on year by year, the shirts being accumulated amongst the possessions of warriors great and low. According to one contemporary source at the time of King Cnut (1016) there were 25,000 mail shirts available in the London Armoury. Even if this is a misprint and a zero has been added in error, 2500 byrnies is a lot of hardware.

Mail shirts became longer as time progressed. Early examples were little more than crotch length with short sleeves. Later, the sleeves reached the elbow and the bottom edge of the garment might be vandyked. Sometimes they were trimmed in brass rings. It is these short shirts that appear to have been referred to as byrnies.

Towards the end of the eleventh century, the mail shirt became longer until it reached the knees or just below with sleeves to the elbow. These long mail garments, often with an integral hood, were split to the groin at the front and back to facilitate riding and could well have taken a year to make. The term 'hauberk', often used to describe these long mail-coats, is derived from the Old English word 'healsbeorg' which originally describes a mail hood (now called a 'coif'); it was not until later that hood and shirt together were known by this name. I have long thought that mail and padding had become one by the end of the eleventh century, the mail being edged in a strip of leather that trapped the edge of the padded garment that supported it.

One might infer from the Bayeux Tapestry that mail 'shorts' were in use, but attempts to replicate these as depicted have proved impossible. This is one of those little puzzles that so occupy the mind of the re-enactor, poor, sad people that we all are!

From the ninth century, head coverings of mail became more common. These would cover the head and neck and probably draped over the shoulders as well. Whilst they are mentioned in manuscript sources, there are no found examples from this period so we can only guess as to their original shape. Padded arming caps would be probably worn under the coif and may also have been worn on their own. A coif-like head covering is shown on figures from Byzantine mosaics, interestingly enough worn by both males and females. By the beginning of the tenth century these had become quite common amongst the professional warriors and during the eleventh century the coif was often integrated with the hauberk becoming a hood. This did away with an unwelcome opportunity for your enemy to slip a weapon into the gap between ventail and shirt. The ventail is a square of mail with its own padding can be attached with rings to the upper chest. This can then be pulled upwards to cover the lower part of the face and secured in position with simple hooks or tied with a leather thong. Although speculative, I think it is the best suggestion so far to explain the 'chest squares' illustrated on the Bayeux Tapestry. They are not universal, but are a good form of protection for infantry and especially the horseman as many of the blows he would encounter would be delivered from below.

Limb armour was far rarer than that used to protect body or head. Whilst a lord of men might have worn mail upon his legs towards the end of the eleventh century, no 'greaves' have ever been found in northern Europe and illustrations of them are unusual. This is a curious anomaly as the lower legs are not protected by a round shield and leg injuries were common. Three ninth-century Danish warriors are illustrated as having strips of some material attached to their legs that reached from knee to instep. One might speculate that this was horn, oil-hardened leather or iron. By the eleventh century the foot too was being covered by some form of armour and wealthier professional warriors were beginning to wear leggings of mail referred to as 'chausses'. These are attached to an arming belt beneath the upper body armour and secured below the knee and above the ankle by small leather straps. This secondary strapping is partly to allow the weight to be shared out along the limb instead of hanging as a dead weight off the hips. In part, the strapping ensures that there is a loose section at the knee without which it is difficult to move quickly.

At this time sleeves in armour were becoming longer and tight-fitting at the wrist. Into the twelfth century, mail mittens began to appear, sometimes as separate protection on a glove back but more frequently as extensions to sleeves. As a subsidiary protection, hardened leather might have been fashioned into 'vambraces' to protect the lower arm and a similar protection used on the lower legs. Alternatively, strips of leather might be wound around both arms or legs to offer some protection.

Whether worn by Norman, Saxon or Viking, body protection varied little throughout Northern Europe.

In closing, I'd like to make the point that an unprotected body will not absorb much punishment from blunt trauma weapons and even less from those equipped with a cutting edge. The unprotected become an immediate target and are swiftly dealt with by armoured fighters. All that we know of combat at this time leads us to the conclusion that the greater part of warfare was conducted by trained, well-equipped fighting men. No doubt the young and the old, the women and the lowest born free men would have done what they could to defend themselves and their families if suffering a direct attack, but it would be unreasonable to think that they would stay and fight when they could run and hide.

1   *Hard times make hard men. English law required every lord to equip his men properly for war. The raiders they faced would have been no less well equipped. (All the warriors depicted in these colour photographs are members of Regia Anglorum and are pictured at public events throughout the UK)*

2   *The dichotomy of the shield-bearing warrior. To make a shot, one must expose one's vulnerable body to the thrusts of the enemy*

3   *A turning point in a battle. This group of warriors has broken through the enemy's shield wall and are pressing home their advantage. Note the mixed use of kite and round shields, common enough around the time of the Conquest*

4   *A defensive shield wall being set up. The front rank drops onto one knee and the second rank stand close behind them. This is fine against a missile storm, but it takes well-trained men to get the unit up and moving quickly*

5 *A planked round shield without cloth or leather facing*

6 *The padded jack or gambuson, the thoracomachus or subarmalis acts as soft body armour or as the basis for mail to be worn over it*

7   *Any form of body armour other than mail was very uncommon. This illustration from the Bayeux Tapestry shows Bishop Odo wearing something unusual. Whatever it is, it is certainly not mail*

8   *The English line at the Battle of Hastings recreated for the BBC television production of* A History of Britain. *Members of Regia Anglorum and Britannia. (Photo: Diane Wall)*

9 *Cymru. A rare set of iron scale armour*

10 *Chausses, leg protection for the post-conquest warrior*

11 *Mailed up to the eyeballs!*

12 *Lameller. Here worn over mail, this form of body protection was very rare in Europe and would have been only available to Vikings who travelled in the east*

13 *The Conquest warrior. The Normans pioneered the use of the horse in warfare in northern Europe. Whilst Saxon and Viking rode their horses to the battle, the Norman did not dismount but used the horse as a moving weapons platform*

14 Hilt furniture took many forms according to fashion and the taste (and wealth) of the user

15 Later hilt furniture

16 *The victors celebrate and the dead lie quietly by. At the end of the day, it's only about killing*

17 *Long hair and straggly beards were unusual. The Norsemen took care of their appearance, plaiting their hair and beards and washing frequently*

18 *This magnificent replica of the Valsgarde 7 helmet is the property of the author and was made by Ivor Lawton. It is one of only seven such replicas*

19 *This instantly recognisable helmet was part of a great treasure hoard buried with (probably) King Readweld on the banks of the River Debden at Sutton Hoo, Suffolk, England, circa AD 650. (Photo courtesy of Richard Underwood)*

20 The author's Coppergate replica is here worn by Gary Waidson

21 This Gjermundbu replica is worn here by Ian Uzzell

22 *The simple pointed helmet was common throughout Northern Europe and is usually referred to with the generic designation 'Spanganhelm'*

23 *They were either of pieced construction and held together with riveted banding or raised from a single sheet of iron. Nasal bars were not uncommon and examples frequently had mail neck curtains or aventails Spangan helms*

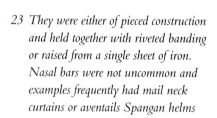

24 & 25

Ships came in all shapes and sizes and small ones could be handled by one or two men, being used for a multitude of mundane tasks. Light and handy, they could be used in the shallowest rivers but were seaworthy enough to be used offshore in reasonable weather conditions.

(One of Regia Anglorum's five ship replicas in use off the Scottish coast)

26 & 27

This is a similar hull to that of the Wreck Three found at Skuldelev and it is not difficult to haul her up as the tide recedes so she can be unloaded in comfort. When the tide floats her off, you need to have a number of strong men who are not afraid to get wet to shove her off. (Members of the Regia Anglorum on the west coast of Scotland with the 'Lord of the Isles' ship replica)

(Cover, this page and top overleaf, photos by Mark Carter)

28 *Slaving was a mainstay of the Norse raiders. Money and moveable goods were best, but a sound male slave was worth over £3500 on the block at Birka — if you could get him there. (Author, far left)*

29 *The raid over and the ship safely at sea on a smiling day, the crew relax and enjoy the sailing, that marvellous feeling of getting something for nothing. (This and previous page, members of Regia Anglorum in the 'Lord of the Isles' ship replica filming for the BBC off the west coast of Scotland)*

30 & 31
The last journey

6 Sword

Praise no day 'til evening;
no wife 'til on her pyre;
no sword 'til tested
no maid 'til bedded
no ice 'til crossed
no ale 'til drunk.

Havamal

To take a sword into your hand for the first time can mean nothing or a great deal. To one, it is the weapon of the true warrior, an extension of reach that has brought us from the caves to the moon and beyond. To another it is just a lump of steel, flattened and sharpened in such a way as to allow one to chop their enemy into several messy pieces, a tool for the working day. Both are accurate, but there can be no dispute that the sword has always been a valued and honoured weapon. A lord of men might require his warriors to swear oaths upon the pommel of his sword and many an agreement has been made, and maintained, with the other end! A father would pass on the weapon that had so often saved his life in battle to his favourite son. A son would receive in awe his father's sword, something that had been honoured and cared for long before he was ever born. It has remains a symbol of power to many people in many times and places. Spears, axes, scramsaexes, bows and arrows can all wound, maim and kill, often with greater efficiency and at less risk to the user than a sword might afford — and cost a great deal less into the bargain. However there is no doubting the great feeling of power and authority that flows into the warrior when he grasps the hilt of a sword.

In the pagan Viking world, everybody knew stories about wondrous blades forged by gods, smiths, giants or dwarves, but very few seemed to know anyone who owned one.

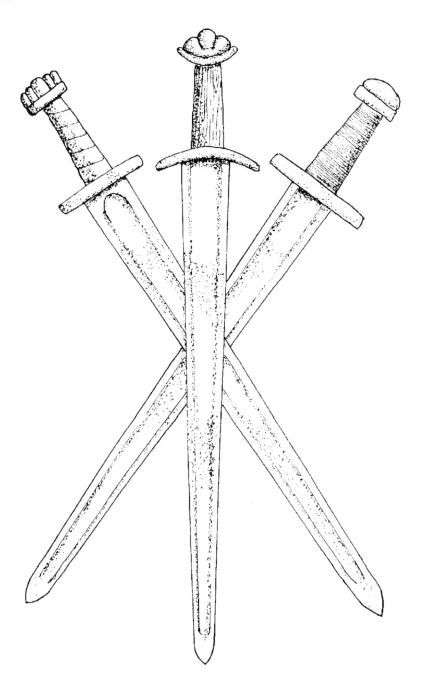

27 *Typical swords from the Viking Age (Levick)*

28 Striking whilst the iron is hot

The practice of naming swords is very old. The Norse myths and sagas are filled with the names of swords, saexes, spears and axes, but swords are, of course, the most important. These are personal names like Magnus Barefoot's sword Legbiter, Olaf Tryggvesson's Quernbiter and less famous ones like Byrnie, Foot, Brain, and Limb Biter, Wolf Tooth, Fierce and so on. The hero Grettir the Strong had a sword called AettarttanXi, rather mysteriously translating as 'Sword of Generations'. Some seem to have been just names, such as Odin's 'Gram' which Sigmund, the Volsung hero, pulled from the roof-tree. Others were descriptive in some way of the sword's appearance or of its qualities.

29 This langsaex must have been a fearsome sight when new (Levick)

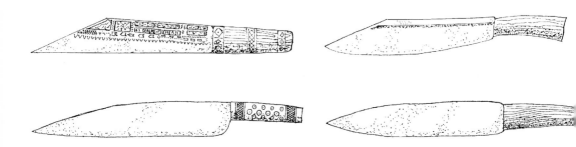

30 Scramsaex came in all shapes and sizes (Levick)

The legend of Sigurd the Dragon Slayer tells of Regin the Smith who made two swords but Sigurd broke them both 'because of his great strength'. Regin then took the shards of the sword Gram, given to Sigmund by Odin himself, and used it to make a new blade. There are two versions of the story. One version says that Regin made a new sword from the best parts of the blades — indicating that he discarded other parts — and another source says that he re-forged the sword Gram from the shards alone. It certainly worked, for Sigmund cut through the anvil on which the sword was forged with one stroke and sheared through a hank of wool carried down against the sword's edge as it floated in a stream.

Getting the impurities out of the iron could be a protracted business. A Norse version of the Welend tales refers to Vollund the Smith who made a sword which turned out to be poorer than he had hoped for. Nothing daunted him for he took a file and reduced the sword to filings that he mixed with corn and fed to his chickens. Over a period of weeks, the whole of the sword passed through his birds, the powerful stomach acid leaching away the impurities. Gathering the fowl's dung, he rendered this down in the fire and retrieved the iron. This he did twice more until finally he had a sword of which he felt proud.

Old swords were perhaps valued not only for their mystical powers (after all, they had taken life) but because only good swords survived to become old swords. A retelling of the tale of one of these famous weapons will give an indication of how they were regarded by the folk who used them. Perhaps the best example of a weapon steeped in myth is Skofnung, the best recorded of all the finer blades to come out of the north. This sword was pattern welded, lived in a wooden box scabbard lined with sheep's wool and had a bag tied over the hilt to protect it from wear and tear. It also had a life-stone with it, a stone or metal bead that was said to offer healing powers to those whom the sword had injured. It

31 A judicial combat (Levick)

first belonged to King Hrolf Kraki of Denmark. Hrolf was very tall and thin, Kraki in old Norse means a pole-ladder, a stout pole with steps sticking out of either side. In the saga of Hrolf's exploits it simply said his sword was 'the best of all swords carried in the Northern lands', and that when he died it was buried with him in his mound at Roskilde.

Some 200 years later the Icelander Skeggi of Vlidfirtlz was passing Roskilde in his ship when he went ashore and broke into the mound of King Hrolf. He took a lot of treasure out of the mound and Skofnung along with it. One might have thought that 200 years underground might not have been the best environment for storing a sword, but it would have been very carefully greased and wrapped before it was put in. Weapons, swords and saexes particularly, were often taken out of graves, sometimes after only a year or two, sometimes decades later. There are even a few which have survived the 1500 or more years to our own day and are in startlingly good condition. Many others have vanished completely of course, but there is a great difference between a spell in the ground of 200 years and one of 1100 or so. Royal graves are not just holes in the ground but are lined with stone or wood like the royal ship burials in Norway. It was no new custom either as the Sutton Hoo ship had a chamber amidships made of stout timber; the king and his hoard sailing through the centuries together before the wood finally rotted and the chamber collapsed. If the chamber had been raided in the tenth century and not in the twentieth, Raedweld's sword might well have been as good as the day it accompanied its owner into the darkness.

When Skeggi broke into the dry, air-tight, stone chamber of Hrolf Kraki's mound, Skofnung was clean, bright and covered in long dried lanolin. One might imagine that he

32 *The core laminations are brought together and twisted together before hammer welding. Note the twists of iron wire to hold the bars in place and hold it all together*

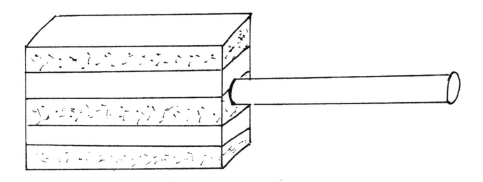

33 *The five laminated layers of iron and steel are mounted on an iron bar*

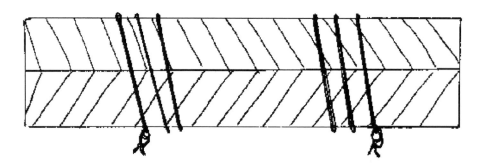

34 *The first two of the core bars are bound together with wire before welding*

did not object to cleaning it though, for a pattern welded sword was a great prize. Skeggi lived in the middle of the tenth century and knew a younger man called Kormak. Now, Kormak thought himself to be something of a warrior and had arranged to fight a duel with Bersi, a professional duelist. He had an iron sword of his own, but thought he would have a better chance against Bersi if he didn't have to stop and straighten it under his foot every third blow. Furthermore, Bersi's sword Hviting had a lifestone with it and Kormack's didn't.

His mother told him that he ought to go to Midfirth to find Skeggi and see if he could borrow Skofnung. Kormac found Skeggi without a lot of trouble and explained his dilemma to the older man. One can imagine him rubbing his chin and looking at his boots as he tried to get out of lending this earnest young man his most valuable possession. He started by telling Kormac that the sword and he were not suited to each other: he said the sword was slow and sure and that Kormac was impulsive and headstrong. Eventually he refused and Kormac went home to his old mum looking gloomy. If you owned a Aston Martin and a young man wanted to borrow it for a race, what would you say?

But like so many strong-minded Scandinavian women, she was not so easily put off. She insisted that he try again and this time Skeggi acquiesced, giving detailed instructions about its use. Luck was an important aspect of all life in the North and it was seen as a special force to be carefully husbanded. Skeggi said that no woman must look upon the blade as it would change its luck. He drew Kormac's attention to the bag that covered the hilt and told him that the sun should not be allowed to shine on it for longer than necessary and therefore it must only be drawn just before use. Even drawing the sword was set about with ceremony. Skeggi said that Kormac must go off to one side when he reached the agreed duelling ground. There, he must take off the bag from the hilt and breathe lightly on the blade as he drew it. This would allow the luck of the sword to swim out in the patterns and — if he was lucky — Kormac would see the snake moving in the fuller.

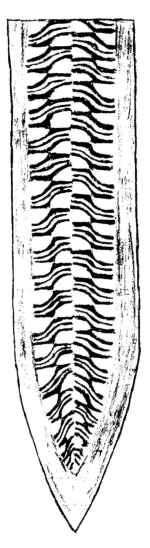

35 *The plain unfullered blade shows the double herringbone of its core structure (Levick)*

Kormac was unimpressed by all this magic nonsense and he laughed at Skeggi, calling him a wizard. Skeggi replied with sinking heart that if he did these things then the fight would go his way — but he was ignored. Arriving home, Kormac was keen to show the sword to his mother, but Skofnung had other ideas and tug though he would Kormac could not drag the sword from its scabbard — although it did howl when the hilt bag was torn off.

36 Shown in scrap cross-section, the eight spirally laminated bars in the core are revealed. At 180 laminations, the edge material is too fine to show any structure

As arranged, Kormac and Bersi rode to the fighting ground with 15 men each. Kormac arrived first and stepped aside, telling his friend Thorgils that he wanted to be alone for a while. He had a struggle to remove the bag and Skofnung was reluctant to fight as it would still not be drawn. Kormac lost his patience with it and put the scabbard under his foot eventually dragging it howling into the light. This poor handling caused the snake to squirm out of sight into the hilt and Skofnung's luck was changed thereafter.

This might seem very fanciful in these pragmatic days at the beginning of the third millennium, but let's consider what this old tale might be trying to tell us. A pattern welded sword is likely to be well made and highly finished. The patterned core of the blade would have been etched with acid, the better to show off the design. The different colours in the layers would show plainly in high contrast to the plain polished flanks of the blade.

Such an expensive blade (perhaps worth as much as £250,000 in our terms, depending to some extent on the hilt furniture) would certainly be contained in a wooden box scabbard and this would have been lined with sheepskin, glued in with the pile facing in and downwards. It was common for the weapon to be tied into its scabbard, although to be fitted with a bag is unusual. The scabbard would be made from two lathes of wood, hollowed out to accept the blade and it would be reasonable for it to be a tight fit in the sheepskin. The lanolin-laden wool wipes the blade with grease every time it is put away. The Balnakeil find reveals that a thin strip of linen was coated in glue and wound around the scabbard in a spiral to keep the two halves together, although other finds show sewn leather covers in addition to rich scabbard fittings to achieve this purpose.

If the scabbarded weapon were to be taken from the relative warmth of a house into the open air, the scabbard might well swell slightly, thus jamming the sword into it. Only a strong pull and twisting force applied to the scabbard would get it out, the wood groaning in protest.

As the blade is dragged into the cold air, breathing on the blade might well cause the patterning to waver and flicker, seeming like a living snake to a willing — and superstitious — mind.

We should remember that we are talking about a sword, and a well-regarded one at that. It was known to have entered the realm of the dead and been brought back by force into the living world. Small wonder then that a folk — who '. . . saw gods behind every rock' as the Christian Saxons said of the pagan Norse people — should look upon this weapon, a widow-maker and drinker of blood, with awe and dread.

Skeggi seems to have been successful in his fight and appears to have kept the sword as Eid, Skeggi's son still had it in the early years of the eleventh century. Being old, Eid

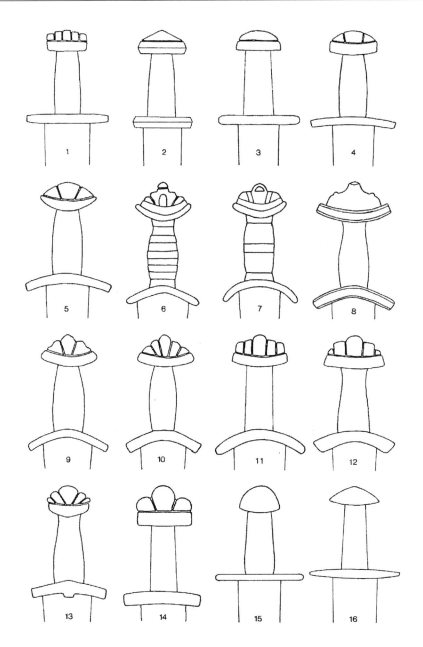

37 The 16 basic styles of Viking Age sword hilt furniture:
1 Viking, ninth century; 2-3 Viking, ninth to tenth century; 4 Viking, tenth century;
5 Viking, eleventh century; 6-9 English, ninth century; 10 English, ninth to tenth century;
11-13 English, tenth century; 14 English, tenth to eleventh century (the most common type in
manuscripts); 15-16 Continental Europe, eleventh century
(Drawings after Levick)

had less use for Skofnung than previously and loaned it to Thorkell Eyjolfsson. Thorkell was engaged in a feud with Grim, an outlaw who had slain Eid's son. Grim and Thorkell fought bitterly at first, but as the formal duel went on they came to realise that they liked each other. Skofnung had bitten into Grim's arm by this time, so Thorkell rubbed the sword's life stone on the wound to speed the healing process. The wound was bandaged and the fight ended there, so Eid didn't get his revenge in the end.

Once again, the sword stayed in the hands of the user, the 'violence' of stealing the weapon from its previous owner being consistent with something that was always used to inflict such extreme violence.

Lucky the sword may have been, but that luck does not seem to have extended to the owner as Thorkell was shipwrecked off Iceland. One might have thought he had other things on his mind as he slid into the freezing water, but his last act was to stick Skofnung into a ship's timber. Perhaps he hoped that it would be carried ashore and pass into another's hand rather than sink beneath the waves to a useless and rusty fate on the sea floor. After a time, the sword was found, recognised and carried to Thorkell's son Gellir and the small island where it came ashore has been called Skofnungsey ever after.

Gellir set out on a pilgrimage to Rome in old age; but in Denmark he was taken ill and died at Roskilde. Skofnung passes from the world at this time, probably in the middle years of the eleventh century. In all likelihood it was buried with him, ironically not far away from the plundered mound of Hrolf Kraki.

> *Wealth dies, kinsmen die,*
> *A man himself must one day die*
> *But this I know well one thing that never dies*
> *Word fame: for word fame never dies for he who achieves it well.*
> (Havamal)

Beginnings

The Viking broadsword represents a significant point in the development of the sword in the western tradition. It should not be looked at in isolation and it is important to consider the weapons that preceded it. It evolved to fulfil certain requirements forced upon the warrior by the style of combat in use at that time. Whilst much combat took place within a shield wall, it is also true that a man may have to fight individual combats, either in battle or to defend himself. When a sword was issued to the soldier in the Roman army, it is likely that it was seen much as the gun has been treated in recent centuries. It appears that whilst the legionary could use his gladius to hack at foes and trees with equal facility, it was not a thing of beauty, decorated with gold and silver. The only thing in his regimented kit that he was allowed to lavish his love and attention on was his pugio, the dagger that sat on his belt by his elbow. When his sword was damaged it was replaced, although its cost was stopped out of his wages if he lost it. It was just a tool to kill Rome's enemies.

In northern Europe, the broadsword developed in a clear line from the Roman cavalry sword, the spatha. Initially of plain iron with wooden hilts and simply furniture, it evolved into a thin, strong blade that was broad — occasionally as broad as 3in (7.7cm) — at the cross guard and tapered to a rounded tip. Although the spatha was frequently of diamond cross section, the broadsword has a broad and deep fuller, a curved depression that tapers with the blade, usually maintaining a cutting edge of about $\frac{3}{4}$in (1.8cm) in depth. The blade might be of plain iron, steely iron or of pattern welded construction, the type of which I have doubt was decided principally according to the depth of the buyer's purse. We will return to this later.

The pommel and cross guard were also variable and first Peterson and later Oakshott devised very sound systems to enable weapons to be dated according to the style of the hilt furniture. When the latter author — the doyen of sword collectors specialising in the Northern tradition — brought out his *The Archaeology of Weapons* over 20 years ago, he quoted the Petersen system which indicates a series of 26 profiles. Sir Mortimer Wheeler simplified the original system into seven basic styles in the mid-1920s and Oakshott added a couple more. These nine basic shapes have stood the test of time remarkably well. Although he modified his classifications a little in *Records of the Medieval Sword* published in 1996, the system is still very largely a workable parameter in the early years of the twenty-first century.

The hilt

It is important for the reader to understand that the pommel and cross guard are not simply present to stop your hand falling off the end and your opponent from loping off your fingers. Made in progressively more massive forms, these items counterbalance the weight of the blade and make it handier in use. This has the effect of making the blade lighter in the hand and a good weapon will balance in the cross guard or just ahead of it and by shifting the balance of the sword, it is possible to decide where the point of best use is situated. In modern parlance, this is called the 'sweet spot' and in a double-edged broadsword with a blade length of about 30in (76cm), this will be about 9in (22.8cm) behind the point. Later developments change this location, but the principal remains the same. I have handled long, two-handed fourteenth-century swords designed to be used from horseback which taper in thickness in such a way as to be thicker at the sweet spot than either side of it. Thus we might make the reasonable assumption that the man who made the sword knew of this phenomenon.

There is a temptation to make the grip of a sword rather long, possibly in the mistaken belief that then one might be able to better use the weapon two-handed in extremity. As swords used throughout Europe in the Viking Age were invariably used in conjunction with a shield, this almost never happens, leaving one with a sloppy grip. Most re-enactors I know prefer a grip to be a tight fit in the hand, making the sword a better extension of reach and contributing to its ease of use.

The grip itself varied enormously in construction and might be lavishly bound in gold or silver wire, fitted with embossed plates or made from alternate bands of precious metal and an organic material like horn. Some were of bone, antler or walrus ivory and other forms might be a simple wooden grip or wood wrapped in leather. Some are fine to look at and make you the envy of your friends, but in the hurly-burly of battle the hand becomes sweaty and that makes a sword's grip slippery if made in any of the above materials. I feel safe in saying this as I have fought on many a sticky summer's day using swords with grips in all the forms described. The Balnakiel Viking grave find in Northern Scotland contained a fine sword which had a wooden grip wrapped in heavy linen thread. This has much to commend it as the surface is grippy without being sticky, and when it becomes slick with dead skin cells, dirt and old sweat, it can easily be stripped off and rewound at little cost and the job completed within an hour or so.

The blade

The blades of swords made and used in the north were all generally similar in shape, although there were exceptions that I will return to later. The blade of a broadsword usually had a length which varied between 26in-32in (66cm-81cm) (as a good average) and this measurement depended mostly on the size, strength and expertise of the user. Almost invariably, the blade would be double edged and taper from about 2.5in (6.35cm) or more at the cross guard and run out to a rounded tip backed up by perhaps 1in (2.5cm) of width just behind the point. A fuller was forged or cut into the iron, a shallow, hemispherical groove that ran almost the full length of the blade and tapered at the same rate, leaving a wedge-shaped cutting edge about ½in (1.25cm) wide. Only at the point and at the cross guard was the blade left full thickness and some swords allowed the fuller to run out under the cross guard itself, which is bad practice. At the widest point of the blade, it is necessary to narrow the top of the blade to form the tang. On a sword made by forging, this would be achieved by heating the iron and drawing it out by hammering. This means that the grain flow of the metal is not compromised and the severe change in section does not guarantee that the weapon will break there, as is so frequently the case with re-enactment swords made today.

The great majority of the work that went into producing a sword 1000 years ago was done by heating the metal and hitting it with a hammer. Only at the closing stages would scrapers, files and polishing compounds, such as fine sand, be used in its production.

There were a few exceptions to the broadsword. The Scandinavians sometimes used a long, narrow-bladed sword that might have been used principally for duelling. Certainly, I cannot see how it would have stood up to the rigours of battle: one good strike with a heavy weapon would have seen it broken or irretrievably bent.

Very few swords have been found with a single cutting edge and these seem to have evolved from a different tradition. I am at pains to separate the falchion from the langsaex but the easiest way is to say that the former has pommel and cross guard like a sword and is sharpened on the curved edge. This weapon may be traced in a separate line of development from the broadsword, beginning with the Ancient Egyptian kopsh and the somewhat later Greek kopis. It continued alongside the broadsword and became the sabre and naval cutlass. You can see one from around the Viking Age in the Castle Museum in Norwich and it is generally referred to as 'The Thorpe Falchion'. The langsaex was a developed and lengthened knife, rarely had hilt furniture other than the grip itself and was sharpened on the straight edge. One was found in the Thames in London and has incised decoration on the blade. It has been well used and has a wicked honed curve to the cutting edge. This is not a tool for the shipwright or the farmer, but a weapon. I have a sharp replica myself and it is quite unwieldy to use, being, of course, very blade heavy. It is quite definitely a weapon and not a tool. Other scrams came in all shapes and sizes even though the basic shape remained the same.

Other traditions

In Islam, the sword was also highly honoured and justly famed for its keenness of edge and strength, the result of the superior eutectic steel employed in its forging. Damascus became the most famed centre of the craft, so that to this day any steel showing a pattern similar to the eutectic steel employed in Islamic swords is called 'damascened'. The smiths in Toledo learned the secrets they needed to make this kind of steel from their Middle Eastern connections and brought its beauty to another field, that of the damascened gun barrel.

At the other extreme, the Javanese kris has far more power as a magical talisman, cultural badge and work of art than it has as a weapon. Meteoric iron is used in some kris not so much for its superior quality or contrasting beauty (although these are valid virtues) but because of its magical associations. Kris are reputed to sigh in disappointment when sheathed, leap into the hand when the owner is attacked and to rattle in the scabbard when danger approaches. Some are even said to have power over fire and be able to raise or put out fires. Even their touch was deadly to their enemies. A cut in the foot from your enemy's kris could kill you.

For the Japanese the sword was venerated for its symbolic and mystical qualities and some of the finer ones were enshrined in Shinto temples. Today, the Japanese sword is seen as a triumph of art and craftsmanship, but during the turbulent years of the Civil Wars, swordsmiths could also hammer them out in quantity. However, there was a price to pay for increased production. Making a good blade takes weeks of concentrated effort and whilst one smithy increased its rate of production from one every two weeks to ten a day, the pattern welded blade vanished until it was re-invented in the twentieth century.

I would particularly like to mention that the methods of pattern welding that the Japanese used were in use in Japan some 700 years after they had been superseded in the west. Considerable nonsense has been spoken and written about the sword of the Samurai and it should be realised that they were no better nor worse than the finest examples of the northern swords made by the same process over 20 generations before. The only thing that one can particularly say in their favour is that they are still being made in more or less the same way that they were made 500 years ago and more. For the filmmaker, the traditional dress, the ceremonies and the painstaking handwork all combine to make excellent camera. This over all other considerations is why the Katana and its ilk are so much better known than the pattern welded Northern European swords in whose path they tread. It is all just a matter of exposure.

Personally, I find them clumsy and one requires considerable practice with the type to use one effectively, as they are single edged and very blade-heavy, the weapon having no pommel and cross guard to balance its weight. If such a sword is designed to be straight, there is no particular reason why a single-edged blade should not twist in the hand during combat. When these blades are tempered, the differential cooling required to ensure a hard edge and a tough but softer core and spine gives a natural curvature to the blade. The smith will take advantage of this curvature to ensure that the tip trails the cutting edge, bringing the balance point behind the centre of gravity. This goes someway to deal with the problems inherent in the use of a single-edged weapon. Being difficult to control, their use dictates a two-handed style that naturally rules out the use of a shield. Therefore, the warrior has to use the sword as a means of defence, imparting great stresses to the blade.

Much is made of the hours of practice that go into making a warrior proficient with a Katana and I would be the last person to disagree that constant effort and daily practice are required to make one proficient with any bladed weapon. However, a good man with a broadsword and in an equal standard of training would find few problems in making his presence felt against such a weapon.

Whilst speaking of curved and single-edged blades, I should briefly mention the familiar scimitar, adapted from the swords of Turkic and other steppe tribes. There is a clear and parallel line of development in these weapons from the Greek falchion. Although far from common, straight, single-edged swords were known in the North and examples exist of Viking swords made in this style.

As I have already indicated, the broadsword can readily be traced back to its roots as a Roman Cavalry weapon, the Spatha. It is important to understand these antecedents before one can look at the broadsword as the lower grade irons available in the North led to the broadening of the blade and the introduction of the fuller.

Originally, this sword was straight sided and of diamond cross-section. The material used was iron, but there is some evidence that a few smiths had recognised that some native iron ores gave a better end product. With the contacts of an extensive empire, the Romans could also import steel from India. It was commonly believed that the small ingots involved originated in China — possibly a deliberately maintained fiction to keep the price high — and they appear to have been used exclusively for the manufacture of such high-priced items as knives and swords, which could then be sold on for great profit.

It is unclear where lamination and pattern welding first appeared. It may well be that the people we have come to call 'the Celts' first thought of it and — like mail — the Romans took the idea on board. In any event, the process was in use by the Romans by the end of the first century after Christ.

The work of the smith

As the last of the Roman high-grade wootz steels became only a memory, Northern smiths turned increasingly to lamination and pattern welding to increase the strength of their products. Iron swords are a liability in battle and we hear in the sagas of warriors withdrawing from the fight ' . . . to straighten their swords under their foot'. In other places, we hear of swords shattering in battle, the pieces flying around the owner's ears. In the North in particular, an imported steely iron sword from the Spanish smiths might break in battle simply because it was made more brittle by the low temperature in which it was being used. It is no stretch of the imagination to consider the reaction of some Dark Age smith when presented with the broken shards of his master's sword. 'Fix this. Make it stronger. It damn near got me killed this time.' How can he achieve his lord's wish? Iron he has, but the steel is beyond his ability to replicate or weld efficiently. However, there is the possibility of combining the two.

Stripping off the hilt furniture, the smith heats the hardwood charcoal-burning fire to a comfortable glow. The forge is curtained from the conditions outside so that the temperature of the fire can be judged more accurately, and visitors are not welcome. The smithy is at the edge of the village away from the vulnerable thatched roofs of the houses. The combination of fire and strange smells, the hammering and cursing and the magic of turning dull blobs of raw iron into a beautiful and terrible weapon all serve to give the smith and his smithy a power and mystery that last to this day. The smith would of necessity be a powerfully muscled man and the lonely nature of his calling would exacerbate his surliness. Who has ever heard of a smith who chats whilst he is working?

The broken pieces of the hard steel blade are heated, hammered and flattened into bar. To these he pays particular attention, heating and drawing them out to three times their original length, then nicking the edge, folding them and twisting them up again. Laminated with three layers of high-grade steel from the broken sword and two layers from his stock, he produces an edge *materiel* that has 15 layers. But he is not content with this. Again they are put to the fire, hammered and twisted to three times their original length. Nicking and folding produces two identical bars of 45 layers: cutting, stacking and welding once more produces a final lamination of 180 layers in a single square bar. The protracted process has reduced the size of the crystalline structure of the steel, aligned the grain structure and reduced the carbon content slightly by oxidisation. The edge will have excellent impact resistance and the tensile strength of the steel has been improved.

High-grade wrought iron of at least two different grades is treated to the same process and these bars set to one side. Even with all the iron readily to hand, to reach this stage might well take him several days of hard, pounding work. He would probably have a young man to help him with the hot metal and another couple of lads to operate the bellows, fetch charcoal and generally keep up with his demands. When there is about 25% more material than the smith needs, he commences the difficult task before him. At best, he will be working within a few degrees of the melting point of the steel and iron as he cannot quite reach a temperature high enough to melt the steel component. His aim is to get both alloys into the closest proximity by heating them and twisting them together in a spiral of iron. He must not overdo it: twisting the bar too tightly would 'wring' the iron, draw out the crystalline structure of the metal too far, making it thin and weak. He reheats the bar time and again, whipping it from the brawling fire and pounding it with a hammer, flattening and welding at the same time as the two alloys hover in a state between solid and liquid referred to as a 'plastic' stage. There must be no flaws in the blade, no 'cold shuts' where the components have not welded; no slag inclusions to separate the layers of iron and steel. It is very highly skilled work and it takes years of experience to be able to produce the stripped bars of pattern welded steel and iron. Steadily he would work on, producing bar after bar of the laminated and twisted iron. Ten would be made in all, each one created from five, seven or nine layers, depending upon the pattern he hopes to create. Five are twisted leftwards and five to the right and he will choose the best eight of them, using the poorer ones for knives or spearheads. When these eight are brought together in the finished sword, they will appear as a herringbone pattern.

But this is only where the story begins, not ends. Having produced the core laminations, he now takes the hard steel bars that he hammered up from the broken sword. Heating and shaping them, he finally attaches them to the core with clamps made from scrap wrought iron, holding them close together. This begins the most crucial part of the welding. A mistake here can ruin days of work, for this is a once-only chance. Too high a temperature could damage the edging material. Too low, and the edge will not weld to the core. Too many blows will distort the precise patterning. He brings them up to welding temperature again, waiting for the first few sparks with their characteristic sparkly texture and colour to rise out of the fire. Although he cannot know it, the billet is around 1090°C. The clamped bars are whipped out of the fire and the smith instantly sets about them, slag and scale flying about him as he works. The lads bring more ashwood charcoal, the best of the burn, dark and hard and literally hand-picked by their master. The apprentice stands ready with this tool or that, or rakes the charcoal away in readiness for the glowing billet to be plunged back into the fire. No-one speaks as the smith wipes the sweat from his brow, staring into the forge for the sparks. Whilst they tell him the metal is hot enough to weld, they also tell him that the iron is beginning to burn, actually being consumed in the oxygen-rich bellowed fire. And the metal must not burn, for burned iron will not weld and has no strength.

Steadily he works on, freeing the clamps from the blade as the welded edge proceeds from the point backwards. When the clamps are finished with he turns the blade this way and that, hammering out the tang from the top of the billet. Hours of work have gone by, the fleeting time slipped passed unnoticed. When the blade is red hot, slag in the iron has a slick look and cold shuts show up as a thin dark line. Behind him in the doorway, his young assistants watch him warily, but he is pleased, smiles to himself and speaks for the first time in hours. 'Ale, lad's that's what I need now!'

All is not lost even if the faults are too great to fix. Knives and spears and axes need shorter blades and as the smith Frank Craddock once said to me: 'I've finished a lot more pattern welded spearheads than I started!'

Tomorrow, he will start again, heating the forge to working temperature and hammering out the fuller, adjusting the thickness of the blade, stretching it here and squashing it there. This process alone will take him a day to achieve. Then with a special tool, a single whetted hard edge set in a shaped piece of wood called an 'old maid's tooth', he will smooth out the fuller and file up the flanks of the blade. Wooden pads loaded with sand follow the grindstones and slowly the sword begins to look like a weapon. The gleaming polished steel is wiped with spirits of vinegar and, if he can get it, lemon juice and the alternate dark and light bars of the patterning start out from the blade. The tang is filed up and polished too, for, in the darkness beneath the grip, terrible cracks can appear in the best of blades. Unseen, they can spread until the blade hangs by a thread, awaiting the next blow before flying apart. But polishing seemed to help — no-one knew why.

The final process in making the blade was hardening and tempering. This critical process was steeped in mystery and a huge range of concoctions and treatments was used at one time or another. Of course, without the benefit of the science of metallurgy, the reasons behind the value of each were not understood and Pliny the Elder attributed these qualities not to the iron but to the water in which the weapons were quenched during hardening and tempering. Whilst it is true that the addition of various salts to the water and its temperature can have some effect on the toughness of the completed blade, the myriad of secret formulas often involving blood, milk, butter, beeswax, whale oil, bear fat and even the living bodies of condemned slaves may or may not have imparted an added strength to a blade. One might reasonably suspect that in a warrior community and particularly amongst a people riven with pagan superstition, the fact that a particular sword had, whilst glowing from the fire, been repeatedly plunged through the body of some luckless human being would add considerably to its value.

The truth though is rather more mundane, in that it is the speed and depth of cooling that controls the hardness and temper of the blade. Having a low boiling point, fresh water cools most quickly and adding salt will slow that process slightly. Oil will cool the steel more slowly still, partly because the boiling point is higher and partly because convection plays a smaller role in getting the heat away from the cooling blade. Carried to its logical conclusion, a resourceful smith might well be producing his best blades in the winter. Cooling the edges momentarily on a block of ice and then plunging the still-glowing blade into a deep vat of thin oil — like refined whale oil, for instance — and violently agitating the fluid to avoid pockets of vaporised oil would have much to commend it.

Few of us are without superstition of any kind, and it is understandable that warriors, who are more exposed to the violent vagaries of luck than most of us, were often of a superstitious turn of mind. Looking to increase the price of his already excellent weapons, the smith might well say that the power of the ice giants and the great whale's spirit had been combined in the making of the sword and recommend that the sword be kept below deck or otherwise out of sight at sea, particularly in the winter.

The cross guard and pommel are made, either by casting or fabrication, silver and gold often being lavished on the hilt. A walrus tusk may be carved to fit the warrior's hand and fitted as a grip, but an experienced fighting man will ask for thin, tarred cord so he can be assured of a better grip when his hands are sweating.

At last, the smith presents the blade to his lord, secure in the knowledge that here is a sword that cannot be bettered, a weapon that, like Skofnung, will outlast him and stride through generations of warriors. Two, three, even four hundred years might pass as his work is handed on from generation to generation, re-hilted, redressed, each incarnation depending upon the original work of the unknown man.

7 Scabbard

I saw the creature crawl away;
It was weirdly wreathed in wonder.

Anglo-Saxon riddle

Swords were expensive and symbols of power and authority. They were also sharp and needed to be kept away from the elements and in such a way as to avoid accidental contact with the cutting edge. All the examples of scabbards identifiable from the archaeological record seem to have been of the box scabbard type, constructed from perishable materials such as wood, cloth and leather. Despite this, substantial physical evidence of their construction remains. Many weapons are encrusted with remnants of the materials of their sheath, preserved by impregnation with corrosive salts from the blade. Organic materials are sometimes also preserved when buried under oxygen-free conditions, such as in the waterlogged soils of the Coppergate urban site at York.

Construction

Scabbards were of rigid multi-layer construction based upon a wooden former and not made from edge- or back-sewn stiff leather alone (**38**).

A thin lath of wood — only $\frac{3}{16}$in (2-3mm) thick in the case of the Cronk Moar sword — was placed over each face of the blade. This was usually lined with sheepskin or some other hide (hair side in), or woollen fabric. The wood was usually covered with leather. The leather covering was usually a single piece, with a butt-stitched seam down the centre of one face (**38a**), or off-centre (**38b**). X-rays revealed that the sheath of the Hedeby sword was riveted instead. Occasionally a cloth binding is found between the wood and leather layers, as in the Ballateare and Cronk Moar finds, although it is unclear whether this was a bandage-like wrapping, or a layer of whole cloth. The Balnekiel find also contained a scabbarded sword. Much fragmented and mineralised, one can nonetheless make out the general construction, which follows that indicated above. However, a thin strip of linen had been wound around the scabbard. There are several turns at the mouth of the scabbard and at the

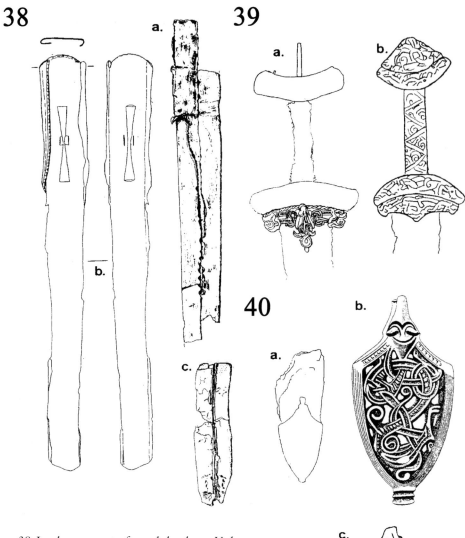

38

39

40

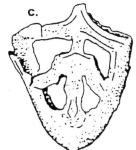

38 *Leather remnants of sword sheaths: a York;*
    b Gloucester; c Durham City
39 *Throat mounts (lockets) found* in situ *on swords:*
    a Dybäck; b Fochtchevataja
40 *Scabbard chapes: a Hafurbjarnastadir (outline*
    only); b York; c L'Ile de Groix

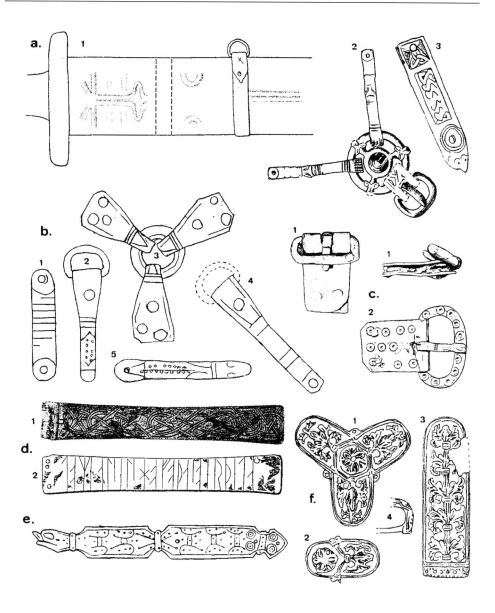

41 Plaques, mounts, buckles and strap ends associated with scabbard finds:

   a Cronk Moar: scabbard and baldric. *1 upper end of scabbard (scale 1:2) showing raised decoration, straps and mount. 2 buckle/strap distributor. 3 strap end.*

   b Ballateare: scabbard and baldric. *1 upper mount. 2 lower mount. 3 strap distributor. 4 loop. 5 strap end.*

   c Repton: *1 buckle from back of scabbard. 2 buckle from waist belt.*

   d Greenmount: strap end. *1 obverse. 2 reverse.*

   e Lund: bone plaque

   f Ostra Paboda: baldric mounts. *1 strap distributor. 2 oval mount. 3 strap end. 4 buckle fragment*

42 *Scabbards in north-western European contemporary art.*

  a *Viking warrior: picture stone, Sockburn, England. Anglo-Danish, ninth to tenth century (Roesdah et al cat. no. F-20).*

  b *Viking duellists: picture stone, Gotland. Scandinavian, eighth century (Humble p65).*

  c *Infantrymen: Golden Psalter, Frankish, ninth century (Humble p50).*

  d *Anglo-Saxons and Normans: Bayeux tapestry, Anglo-Norman, late eleventh century (Stenton, pl. 12, 70).*

  e *Warrior: fragmentary stone frieze from Winchester Old Minster, Anglo-Saxon, eleventh century (Roesdahl et al 1981m ca. no. J-1; Gravett p28)*

  f *'Goliath': MS Cotton Tiberius, Anglo-Saxon, c.AD 1050 (Gravett pl. 11).*

  g *Earl Harold's scabbard on waist belt: Bayeux tapestry (Stenton, pl. 11).*

  h *Charles the Bald's bodyguard.* Vivian Bible, *Frankish c.AD 846 (Hubert et al pl. 129)*

tip and a neat spiral of cloth is wound around the centre section. Either on top of or beneath (it is impossible to be sure) this binding is a separate layer of linen, thus entirely covering the wood. No doubt the cloth was glued to the wood originally and the reconstructed scabbard gained considerably in strength from the application of this thin layer of cloth. The throat may have been reinforced with a leather binding strip; the remains of one were found on the Cronk Moar sword, and a strip was also indicated by stitch holes on the York sheath. Metal throat mounts (lockets) decorated to match the sword hilt are occasionally found (**39a** & **39b**). The tip of the scabbard was presumably tapered, and was sometimes fitted with a metal chape, usually of openwork bronze (**40a-c**).

A leather sheath remnant from Gloucester (**38b**) may represent a different, non-rigid type of construction. The inside bears the mark of a longitudinal metal(?) strip near the opening, where the presumed supporting strap was inserted, which may have been to stop the mouth of the sheath flopping over when the sword was withdrawn. Alternatively, this

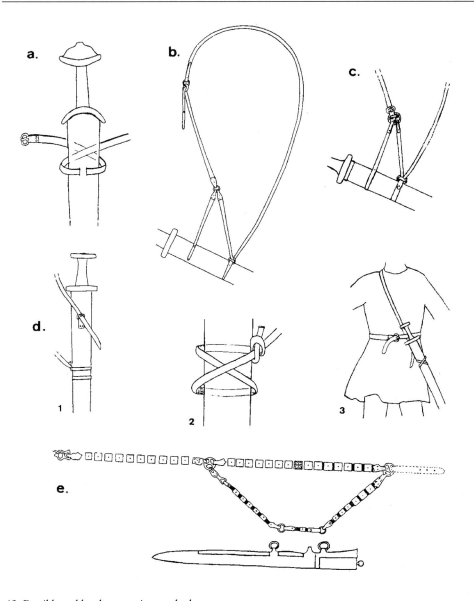

43 *Possible scabbard suspension methods.*

  a Gloucester. Suspension from a looped belt (or baldric).

  b Ballateare baldric after Bersu and Wilson (1966).

  c Cronk Moar: variant on Ballateare reconstruction. Partly after Bersu and Wilson (1966).

  d Repton. 1 Rear view: strap adjusted by buckle near throat of scabbard, a second suspension
  point lower down to hold the scabbard clear of the legs. 2 Possible method of lashing lower
  suspension point. 3 How the scabbard may have been worn: suspension from
  baldric with waist belt fastened over it.

  e Mikkola. Horizontal suspension at the right-hand side from a secondary loop of a waist belt.
  The outline of a long Swedish knife in a bronze-mounted sheath (from Vendel, tenth century)
  is shown in position (approx. to scale). Black = surviving leather

may simply be the outer covering of a standard wooden scabbard, with the metal reinforcing the attachment point of a belt or baldric.

Decoration

Given the Viking taste for the ornate, we can presume that many scabbards were richly decorated. However, apart from metal lockets and chapes, little remains. The leather covering of the Cronk Moar scabbard was decorated with moulded designs (**41a**). Plaques of bone (**41e**) or other materials may have been riveted to scabbards; rich pre-Viking finds from Vendel include scabbard mounts and plaques of gilt bronze (eg. Humble 1989 p.61).

Suspension

Most contemporary illustrations indicate that swords were slung at the waist, either in a near-horizontal position (**42a-c**) or at a steeper angle to the rear (**41d, e & f**). The scabbard might depend from a shoulder harness (baldric, **42f**), or have been attached near the mouth to a waist belt, perhaps by a button passing though a slit in the belt (**42g**), or by a looped strap (**42d & f**). Such a strap might have passed through the two slits in the Gloucester sheath (**43a**). Possible reconstructions of the Ballateare and Cronk Moar scabbards have the swords suspended nearly horizontally, from complex baldrics (**43b & c**). The Repton sword was found lying on edge along the left leg of the skeleton, from toe to hip. If this was its position in life, it indicates a vertical or near-vertical suspension. The small buckle (**41c**) attached to the back of the scabbard presumably adjusted a suspension strap. It might have hung either from a waist belt (for which a buckle was found) or a baldric, perhaps with the waist belt fastened over it to keep the baldric in place (**43d**).

Frankish trefoil strap mounts (**41f**) were favoured by Viking looters as gifts for their women, though it is possible that some were used for their original purpose (**42h**). Eastward-faring Vikings were influenced by the dress of nomadic peoples such as the Magyars, whose Hungarian-style belts with mounts for horizontal suspension of a sword or large knife have been found in Swedish and Finnish graves (**43e**).

Discussion

It is surprising that scabbards were of such apparently fragile construction, given that contemporary art indicates that they were worn into battle. However, this will only apply if the wooden part of the scabbard is not supported by secondary layers of linen and leather. The secret of its strength lies in the composite nature of its construction. Though they could be broken if fallen on, I suspect (or certainly hope) that this happened far less frequently to the medieval warrior than his modern re-enactor counterpart. A far greater drawback of the rigid scabbard is its tendency to get tangled in the wearer's legs at a vital moment. It must have been crucial to suspend it correctly in order to prevent this. The horizontal suspension method which predominates in Viking art would appear to best satisfy this requirement. A vertically-slung scabbard would scarcely be practical for walking, let alone fighting, and indeed nearly all of those shown on the Bayeux Tapestry are sloped back clear of the legs (e.g. **42d**). It would be interesting to hear from anyone who has experimented with different methods.

Select catalogue

Swords with associated scabbard remnants of Scandinavian origin

Ballateare, Man: Sword, grave find *c*.AD 900. l. 3ft 1.5in (95.5cm) overall, 2ft 7in (80.2cm) blade. Remnants of composite scabbard: wood lined with textile and bound with tabby weave cloth, then leather. Transverse copper alloy mounts, l. 1.85in & 2.10in (47mm & 54mm), 4.75in and 9.8in (*c*.12cm & 25cm) below guard, with remnants of leather suspension straps, 6in-7in (1.5-1.8cm) wide (*see* **41b**). Associated three-way strap all probably from baldric (**43b**). Ref. — Bersu & Wilson 1966.

Brandstrup, Denmark: Sword, grave find AD 950-1000. l. 3ft 2in (97.5cm) overall, 2ft 9in (83.5cm) blade. Remnants of wooden scabbard with traces of fine cloth binding at the tip. Shanks of two iron nails or rivets which are probably suspension points. Two small rectangular iron (belt?) fittings lay near the sword. Refs. Lavrsen 1960; Roesdahl et al. 1981 cat. no. H-1).

Cronk Moar, Man: Sword, grave find *c*.AD 900. l. 3ft 1.5in (95cm) overall, 2ft 7in (79cm) blade. Remnants of composite scabbard: wood (oak) lined with textile and bound with linen, then hardened leather with moulded designs (*see* **41a**). Transverse copper alloy mount below guard with remnants of leather strap (**41a**). Remains of two other straps only on back of scabbard: at mouth (reinforcing?) and 2.75in (*c*.7cm) below guard. Associated copper alloy three-way strap distributor/buckle (ring with cabochon glass inlay) and strap-end l. both probably from baldric (**41a**). Ref. Bersu & Wilson 1966.

Donnybrook, Ireland: Sword, grave find ?ninth century. Traces of wooden scabbard lined with animal skin, probably sheepskin. Ref. Hall 1978.

Dyback, Sweden: Sword, single find AD 950-1000. Elaborate scabbard locket, gilded and nielloed silver, w. 3in (7.9cm). Moulded decoration in the Danish late Jellinge-Mammen style, the upper edge is finished with twisted gold wire. Refs. Graeme-Campbell 1980 cat. no. 250; Roesdahl et al. 1981 cat. no. K-3; Roesdahl & Wilson 1992 cat. no. 414.

Fochtchevataja, Ukraine: Sword, early eleventh century. Scabbard locket, bronze w. 3.5in (8.8cm). Moulded decoration in variant Ringerike style matches pommel and guard (**3b**). Refs. Roesdahl & Wilson 1992 cat. no. 311, Kirpicnikov 1969.

Hafurbjarnastadir, Iceland: Sword, grave find AD 950-1000. Remains of composite wooden scabbard enclosing tip of sword, mouth gilded bronze openwork chape decorated in Jellinge style, l. 3in (8.2cm). Refs. Graeme-Campbell 1980 cat. no. 273; Roesdahl & Wilson 1992 cat. no. 324).

Haithabul Hedeby, Germany: Sword, from the boat grave *c*.AD 850. Traces of riveted leather sheath with fur lining. Refs. Graeme-Campbell 1980 cat. no. 249; Roesdahl & Wilson 1992 cat. no. 171.

Repton, England: Sword, grave find AD 873(?). l. 2ft 11in (89.7cm) overall, blade 2ft 6in (77.3cm). Remnants of composite scabbard, wood lined with hairy hide (sheepskin?) and bound with leather. Copper alloy buckle on back face of scabbard 3.35in (*c*.8.5cm) below guard, orientation uncertain, probable suspension point (**43d**). Copper alloy belt buckle also found at waist (**41c**). Refs. Biddle & Kjolye-Biddle 1992; Roesdahl & Wilson 1992 cat. no. 352.

Skerne, England: Sword, river (ritual?) deposit, ninth-tenth century. Remnants of wooden (willow poplar) scabbard, with fibrous lining, possibly fleece. Ref. Dent 1984.

Leather sheath fragments

Durham City, England: Tip of leather sheath, urban site tenth-eleventh century. Oxhide, l. 7in (*c*.18.0cm), w. 2in (*c*.4.8cm). Central butted seam on one face, tapered at one end, which has stitch holes for a (missing) repair patch or reinforcement (Fig. 2c). Ref. — Carver 1979.

Gloucester, England: Leather sheath, urban site ninth century. Upper part of slightly tapering sheath, l. 2ft 6in (78cm), w. 3in (8cm) at mouth. Butted seam down one face, off centre. On other face two slits, probably for suspension strap. Between these, the impression of an hourglass-shaped stiffener (missing), l. 5in (12.5cm). Opening dressed with edge-flesh stitches, curvature corresponds to drooping quillions of late Anglo-Saxon swords. Ref. Heighway et al. 1980.

York, England: Parts of two leather sheaths, urban site tenth century. The first (550) in three fragments, total l. 2ft 5in (72.4cm), w. 2.3in (*c*.6cm). Slightly tapering with central butted seam on one face. Smaller stitch holes at the remaining top edge and extending 1.5in (4cm) down one side may have attached a binding strip at the scabbard mouth, the impression of which remains (**2a**). The second sheath (681) is similar but much less complete, l. 1ft (32cm,) w. 2.3in (6cm). Ref. MacGregor 1982.

Other items

Greenmount, Ireland: Strap end, single find *c*.AD 1100. Oblong strap end, Copper alloy with interlaced silver and niello inlay. One end is split to take a leather strap, originally held by two rivets. Reverse has runic inscription: tomnalselshofopasoerpesa = 'Domnall Seals-head owns this sword' (**41d**). Ref. Roesdahl & Wilson 1992 cat. no. 405.

L'Ile de Groix: Chape: ship cremation AD 900-50. Bronze, l. An eagle is outlined in openwork. Refs. — Du Chatellier & Le Pontois 1908-9; Price 1989; Roesdahl & Wilson 1992 cat. no. 360.

Lund, Sweden: Scabbard(?) mount, urban site AD 1000-50. Polished bone, l. in form of a dragon, with carved decoration. Three rivet holes, rivets missing (**41e**). Ref. Roesdahl & Wilson 1992 cat. no. 577.

Mikkola, Finland: Remains of belt, grave find eleventh century. Bronze-mounted leather belt w.0.75in (*c*.1.8cm) with dependant loop for suspending a [missing] item such as a weapon or purse. Estimated length of main belt 2ft 7in-2ft 9in (80-5cm). The remaining bronze mounts consist of 28 larger and 9 smaller square plaques fastened to the leather by a central rivet; two spoked d. 1.3in (*c*.3.4cm) and two three-way strap distributor rings; six animal-headed and six other strap terminals; and a buckle. Magyar influence, but made in Scandinavia (**43e**). Ref. Roesdahl & Wilson 1992 cat. no.225, see also no.132.

Ostra Pdboda, Sweden: Set of Frankish baldric mounts, buried hoard ninth century. Silver with gilt and neillo. Trefoil strap distributor 1.4in (9.8cm); two oval mounts l. 2.50in (6.3cm); strap end and a fragment of belt buckle (**41f**). Ref. Roesdahl & Wilson 1992 cat. no. 135.

York, England: Chape, single find tenth century. Cast copper alloy, l. 3.4in (8.6cm). Openwork decoration in Jellinge style. Refs. Graeme-Campbell 1980 cat. no. 274 — see also 275; Hall 198X; Roesdahl & Wilson 1992 cat. no. 374 — see also Nos. 217, 263, 310, & 330.3.

8 Helmet

Wordlessly, his wife brought him his war-helm.
He took it from her and stripped
off its bag. It was heavy in his hand,
the polished iron gleaming dully in the morning light.
He turned it over in his hands,
each dent, nick and mark reminding him
of what he had done and where he had been.

From 'For the Lands Weal' book one

If we base a supposition upon found examples, helmets were extremely rare in the Viking period. Even if we extend the supposition to include tertiary evidence it is hard to support more than about 20 percent of a field force wearing head coverings specifically designed as wargear. From our modern perspective of safety first, this seems to be nothing short of foolhardy, but it does appear on the face of it that many, many warriors went into battle with nothing but their hair between them and the enemies' weapons. Common sense dictates that this could not have been the case as it would make instant victims of the bare headed.

I have long felt that the older style of visored and crested helmet remained in use for much longer than is commonly accepted today. As helmet design progressed through the Viking age, helmets became lighter and more functional and crested helmets seem to have been phased out by AD 1000, although there are quite late references to them in various carvings, coins and manuscripts. The cross shafts at Brompton in north Yorkshire, Sockburn and Chester-le-Street, Durham all illustrate warriors wearing helmets of rounded form with crests, the one at Sockburn being particularly prominent. The mid-

44 *Figures wearing pointed helmets from (l-r) the Fre figure from Rallinge, lund in Sweden, the Ledberg runestone and the antler*

eleventh-century illustration of David and Goliath in the Cotton MS Tiberius C. VI show a variety of views of a pointed helmet with a beaded brow band and lateral band. Considered together, they indicate that the lateral band must be proud of the cap of the helmet. There is another, older, manuscript in the Leningrad museum showing David killing Goliath (with a sword, incidentally) and David is actually pulling the giant's head forward by the crest on his helmet. The picture was probably drawn in Northumbria or Ireland and the helmet is typically a crested Anglo-Saxon helmet.

An eleventh-century coin of Aethelred II of England issued between AD 1003 and AD 1009 shows the king wearing a crested helmet, possibly in the Roman fashion. It is possible, therefore, that crested helmets were manufactured and in use in an unbroken line from the fifth to the tenth centuries, finally falling out of favour around the turn of the millennium as the more practical pointed helmets came into use.

If ever there was a folk sunk in their own myth, it was the Vikings. One need only look at the way the sagas celebrated the violence and individual militarism inherent in their culture, and at the organisation and maintenance of the super-militaristic camps of the Jhomsvikings and at Treleborg, Fyrkat, Aggersborg and Nonnebakken. Tradition still plays a big role in the military establishment even in the pragmatic modern age and the physical symbols of bitter defeats and celebrated victories are treasured long after the event has become little more than a folk memory. Until the Victorian antiquaries started touring country churches buying up achievements of arms in the 1800s, England was littered with these solid memories of past glories. Even in civilian life, there is no reason to look askance at this idea. If we look for a parallel in the modern world, we might use a Georgian silver teapot for its original purpose, a Tudor chest for storing blankets or Victorian dining chairs to sit to table. With such a paucity of finds we might very well suspect that helmets were so valuable (circa £5300 according to a contemporary Central European list) as to be worn by successive owners until they just rusted through across the brow and were dismantled to re-use their valuable iron. Therefore, I include earlier helmets in this chapter with this idea specifically in mind.

Early helmets from Sutton Hoo and the stylistically similar Valsgarde and Vendel sites are loosely based upon Roman cavalry officers parade helmets. Of the found examples

45 An example of the 'Phrygian Hat' from Ms. Cotton. Claudius.B.IV in The British Library. As a design it is completely uncorroborated by any finds in Europe

from the archaeological record, the group of Valsgarde and Vendel (*c.* seventh century) period helms are the largest group to survive the last thousand years or so. Dating to the middle years of the fifth century, they are similar in concept and artistic style to the British Sutton Hoo (*c.* seventh century) helmet, the British Museum replica of which being probably the most recognisable of all European helmets.

Others are the Deurne helmet from the Netherlands, the Benty Grange (*c.* mid-seventh century) from Derbyshire, the Ulltuna (*c.* early eighth century) from Sweden, the Anglian helmet (*c.* mid-eighth century) found at Coppergate in York, the Pioneer Helmet found in Northamptonshire, the Gjermundbu (*c.* mid-tenth century) from Sweden, the Morken from Belgium, the Kiev helmet, a few Spanganhelms(*c.* ninth/tenth century) from Germany and the Wenceslas helm from Czechoslovakia. Whilst this is not an exhaustive list, there are not many more examples.

All the rounded style of helms are based upon a series of iron bands that are riveted together to form an open frame. These are then infilled with iron plates in most cases, but it is possible that some of the Vendel helms and the Benty Grange helmet were infilled with shaped plates of horn or *cuir bouilli* (leather boiled in beeswax), but not quite as the replica in the Sheffield museum would suggest. It is also possible that basketwork helms covered in hide or leather were used but, again, none have survived, although there is an earlier Scandinavian find of a metal 'basketwork' skullcap which may have been worn over a soft covering. Some of the Valsgarde helmets feature interwoven iron strips, riveted where they cross and at the brow band. This type of construction is very clearly seen in

46 These two photos indicate current thinking on the 'chest square' illustrated on the Bayeux Tapestry. On the left, it is undone and lies flat upon the chest exposing its leather lining. On the right, it is shown fastened, thus protecting the neck

the Ulltuna helmet which is in a remarkable state of preservation.

The Anglian helmet from Coppergate was found in York and narrowly escaped being destroyed by the mechanical digger that uncovered it. Although constructed two generations before the Viking age started in Britain, it appears still to have been in use in Jorvik during Viking times. When discovered in the remains of a well, one of the cheek flaps had been carefully removed along with the neck curtain. Perhaps it had been stolen from the armourers' workshop and thrown away when the thief saw how distinctive it was — we shall never know. It is certainly the finest helmet found in Britain and added much to our knowledge of the mail making and helmet construction techniques of our ancestors.

The construction of the Kiev helmet is unlike any other. A series of 14 sub-triangular strips are held at the apex by a pair of oval plates between which they are trapped and riveted. At the lower edge, a series of large, rounded washers are used to spread the riveted load, there being one washer and rivet at either side of each strip. There is no other riveting. The helmet is bowl shaped with ear cut outs at the rim and there is no nasal bar.

The Norwegian Gjermundbu helmet is the only one that we can honestly say was a

Viking helmet, although many other styles are depicted in carvings and manuscript sources. The addition of a spectacle visor might seem to give better protection to the eyes and upper face. Unfortunately, the iron faceplate merely serves to direct thrusts into the eyes, certainly not what the designer intended.

The Spanganhelms are from a different family and are of a pointed profile. Early examples were constructed by framing and riveting in the same way as their more rounded cousins. Later types were hammered from a single sheet of iron and often had a nasal bar riveted on. They were sometimes worn with a mail aventail, and a padded arming cap may well have been used. There is an intermediate style where the sections are riveted together without framing as the users found that their pointed profile gave them a greater inherent strength. These helmets were in use from about AD 850 and were still being made in this style in the twelfth century .

An iron helmet is of little use on its own. It must not be too close-fitting as it will then transmit the shock of a blow from a weapon direct to the skull of the wearer. All helmet finds indicate some form of shock protection, sometimes by means of padding and sometimes by way of a series of leather straps riveted to the inside of the rim and tied in the dome with a thong. The Sutton Hoo helmet is huge and must have had a lot of padding inside to bring it down to normal head size. Perhaps it used both methods. Separate padding might be used too and various of my helmets have provision for a padded arming cap and room for a mail hood or coif as well; in another case, a skull cap of heavy woollen felt which can be worn separately. I also have a leather hat made of greased elk skin that offers some protection in itself and it actually fits nicely inside the webbing of my Valsgarde Seven replica.

Another use of padding was the distribution of weight. These big iron helmets are heavy, particularly those — like the Valsgarde, Vendal and Sutton Hoo — which are covered in copper alloy tinned pressings and bronze decoration. With the addition of mail neck protection, they may weigh ten pounds (4.5kg) or even more.

Padded hats might well have been used by poorer warriors as primary protection and it is possible that the curious 'Phrygian caps' illustrated by Anglo-Saxon artists in a military context are examples of this. The only surviving helmets in the 'phrygian' style are fourth-century BC Greek. Only 1400 years and 1200 miles out; unlikely as it may seem to us it might well be a long-perpetuated copyists error based upon Roman illustrations.

Early helmets frequently had cheek flaps, but these seem to have dropped out of favour quite quickly. All war gear tends to evolve more and more simplistic types, form giving function as they say. Cheek flaps might offer you greater protection from side blows to the head but they are hot and uncomfortable to wear if done up tightly. They also deafen you, squeaking and clattering in a most irritating fashion as you move about if you leave them undone.

It is just possible that cheek flaps gave rise to that most clichéd aspect of Viking lore, the horns on helmets syndrome. Long years ago, whilst preparing for combat, I noticed someone in the line of approaching warriors that apparently had horns or wings on his helmet. I was surprised, because even in the early 1980s, there was only the occasional die-hard poser who still dared to wear horns as social peer pressure had made all but the most obstinate get rid of them. When the man got closer, I could see that he had tied up his cheek flaps to stop them banging about, it being a hot day. I hasten to add that I do not espouse this as a reason, only that it made me look hard after an initial impression.

Thick leather was possibly used to make helmets although there are no finds whatsoever of protective head coverings being made from anything other than iron in this period. However, the technique of 'cuir bouilli' or scalding the leather in boiling water or very hot beeswax to make it stiff and hard was known at the time and may have been used to manufacture non-metallic helmets. It has been suggested as an alternative for the iron plates inside the frame of early helmets. Thick leather can be riveted successfully to a frame and is very good at deflecting glancing blows although it may be penetrated by heavy direct thrusts or blows.

Helmets sometimes had a 'curtain' of mail called an aventail, hanging from the back of them to protect the back of the head and neck. In early times this was sometimes made from not mail but solid iron strips that hung from the rim of the helmet, something that would not, I fancy, encourage the wearer to do much running. Mail coifs (coif from the Late Latin '*cofia*' — a helmet and the Old French '*coife*' — a head dress) or 'healsbeorgs', were worn from the ninth century and tended to cover the top and back of the head, the cheeks, chin, neck and perhaps some of the shoulders. Again coifs are mentioned but have never been found, so we can only guess as to their original shape. By the beginning of the tenth century these had become quite common amongst the professional warriors. By the eleventh century the coif was often integrated with the hauberk becoming a hood.

The 'ventail' section of mail on or near the chest that folds up over the neck and chin, and hooked into position over the lower face, is the best explanation for the shapes found on the knights armour in the Bayeux tapestry. They are not universal, but seem to be a sensible protection for a horseman, as most of the attacks he would receive would come up from below. Padded arming caps would be probably worn under the coif and may also have been worn on their own. The coif as a head covering is shown on figures from Byzantine mosaics, interestingly enough worn by both males and females. How widely they were worn elsewhere as normal headgear is unknown until the Middle Ages.

The helmet was part of the panoply of the properly equipped warrior and it would have been a rare man indeed that went willingly to war without something between his naked scalp and the blows of his enemies.

9 Money

Across the turn of the first millennium, the tribute ships were coming from Scandinavia every year to demand money of the English to go away: 16,000lb (7273kg) in 994, 24,000lb (10,909kg) in 1002, 36,000lb (16,363kg) in 1007 and 48,000lb (21,818kg) in 1012. However such figures are generally meaningless. Does it fill a small van? A large lorry? In modern terms it represents about 56 metric tonnes of silver and had a value at that time of something in the order of £1,200,000,000. Suffice it to say that it probably equalled the entire tax revenue of the State in any two-year period. England was buying peace and simultaneously paying for further Viking raids with her own money. The effect in Scandinavia was galvanic. Ships were built with the sole intention of getting ever larger numbers of warriors across the narrow sea in the mad scramble to share in the rain — nay, storm — of silver that came back year by year to Scandinavia.

Although it seems weak of the English State to have paid out such huge sums, there is reason to believe that it was actually cheaper to pay than to call out the army (who would need to be paid) and fight a difficult war against a tenacious foe who, even if beaten, would be back again next year. Indeed, the sums extracted from England were so huge that it proved — in an age where there were precious few things one could spend one's money on — impossible to spend it all and much of the coin was simply buried in hoards to be discovered by gleeful metal detectorists, cheerful farmers and disappointed dogs in recent times. Many of the Anglo-Saxon coins on display in the museums of the world are uncirculated, having been taken from coin hoards in Scandinavia.

A thousand years ago, the monetary system was far removed from the sophisticated and complex world in which we live today. In principal, although everything had a value,

47 Greedy men? No more than any other

48 Saxon coin

unless something unexpected (and usually unpleasant) happened, the bulk of society operated on the barter system. Coins in the hands of ordinary folk would have been unusual and many small coin-finds show that the coin was bent in half, probably around a leather thong for safety.

In England, the only coin in general circulation was the silver penny. It was quite common to cut coins in half or in quarters, something entirely necessary in a system based upon one coin. The Norse term 'forthing' entered the language to define the smallest coin in later circulation, the farthing. It was of very pure metal and was kept that way by a series of draconian legal measures designed to remove bits of the moneyer's body with sharp implements if he showed a predilection for adding a little lead to his silver or trimming them too closely. It was this that the Vikings came for. Minted silver coin was slightly more valuable than the simple weight as English money was accepted all over Europe — something else that has changed with the passing years. Whilst you will find mention of pounds and shillings, these are accounting terms only and the coins did not exist.

One of the most difficult problems is trying to sort out just what something was worth even in contemporary relative terms, let alone a modern equivalent. There are many variables and these depended to some extent on where in Europe you lived, and our available references date over several centuries from the seventh to the eleventh century. Although inflation was very slow and famine and glut would have played a part, it is possible to make a sensible stab at comparative values.

In its simplest form early English money was divided into pounds, shillings and pence, but the subdivisions were not the same as our pre-decimal coinage that was in use up until 1971. The pound in use was the Troy pound (approx 11.5 modern ounces or 373g) divided into 240 pennies (making a Saxon penny about 1.55g). The shilling did not have a constant value, varying from 4-6 pence, not the more recent 12 pence. To attempt to make sense of it all, I will average the value of a shilling to be worth 5 pence with 48 shillings to the pound. The pound referred to was that of weight and represented a pound of silver. Whilst the forgoing is rather simplistic, it does give us somewhere from which to make a start.

It is necessary to get some kind of idea as to what the coinage and prices convert to in modern terms. A straight conversion to silver as bullion gives a silver penny a value of about 25-30 pence and a pound of silver about £60-72. However the relative value of silver today is very much lower today than in the Viking Age. The staples of life are a better yardstick and one can draw parallels from the price of corn, ale, bread or a soldier's pay. Depending on which figures you use, a Saxon penny might be worth anything from £10-200, although most methods give a value in the range of £20-50. During these times, England was relatively prosperous apart from the depredations of the Vikings, so a conversion rate on the low side seems appropriate. 1 Saxon silver penny = £20, 1 shilling = £100 and 1 pound = £4800. Although not entirely accurate, it is probably as good as one can estimate given the range of variables we have to contend with.

In the following tables, the value is given in early English pounds (l), shillings (s) or pence (d), weight of silver (g) and modern pounds sterling (£). After each item a letter will indicate whether the price comes from Britain [B], Western Europe [W], Central Europe [C], Northern Europe [N] or Eastern Europe [E].

King's Hunting Dog, untrained	[B]	120d	186g	£2400
King's Hunting Dog, 1 yr old	[B]	60d	93g	£1200
King's Hunting Dog, young	[B]	30d	46g	£600
King's Hunting Dog, pup with unopened eyes	[B]	15d	23g	£300
King's Lap Dog	[B]	1l	372g	£4800
Stranger's or Dunghill Dog	[B]	4d	6g	£80
Old Swarm of Bees	[B]	24d	37g	£480
Ox	[E]	80.5d	125g	£1610
Ox	[C]	88.5d	137g	£1770
Virgin Swarm of Bees	[B]	16d	25g	£320
Swarm of bees from a second swarm	[B]	8d	12g	£160
Swarm of bees from Virgin Swarm	[B]	12d	18g	£240
Second Swarm of Bees	[B]	12d	18g	£240
Sparrow Hawk Nest	[B]	24d	37g	£480
Unfledged Peregrine	[B]	120d	186g	£2400
Unfledged Sparrow Hawk	[B]	12d	18g	£240
Pig	[E]	20d	30g	£600
Sheep	[E]	10d	15g	£300
Male Slave	[N]	197.5d	306g	£3,950

Arms and Armour

Helmet	[C]	53s	410g	£5300
Mailshirt	[C]	529d	820g	£10,580
Shield and Spear	[C]	88.5d	137g	£1770

Spear	[W]	33d	51g	£660
Sword	[W]	81.25d	126g	£1625
Sword	[B]	240s	1860g	£24,000
Sword and Scabbard	[C]	308.5d	478g	£6170

Fines, etc.

Accepting service of another's ceorl	[B]	120s	930g	£12,000	
Binding an innocent ceorl	[B]	10s	77g	£1000	
Binding an innocent ceorl and shaving him like a priest	[B]	60s	465g	£6000	
Ceorl entering into illicit union	B]	50s	387g	£5000	
Ceorl neglecting fyrd duty	[B]	30s	232g	£3000	
Ceorl seeking new lord	[B]	60s	465g	£6000	
Failure to perform fyrd duty	[B]	40-50s	310-387g	£4000	
Fighting (not in war)	[B]	120s	930g	£12,000	
Freeman working on Sunday	[B]	60s	465g	£6000	
Holding a woman's breast	[B]	5s	39g	£500	
Landless thegn neglecting fyrd duty	[B]	60s	465g	£6000	
Not baptising child within 30 days of birth	[B]	30s	232g	£3000	
Ordering a slave to work on Sunday	[B]	30s	232g	£3000	
Priest working on Sunday	[B]	120s	930g	£12,000	
Raping a female slave	[B]	65s	504g	£6500	
Removing a nun from a nunnery without permission	[B]	120s	930g	£12,000	
Reward for catching thief	[B]	10s	77g	£1000	
Seducing a free woman	[B]	60s	465g	£6000	
Thegn entering into illicit union	[B]	100s	775g	£10,000	
Thegn neglecting fyrd duty	[B]	120s	930g	£12,000	(+ land)
Throw a woman down but not lie with her	[B]	10s	77g	£1000	
Violation of an archbishop's protection	[B]	3l	1116g	£14,400	
Violation of bishop/eolderman's protection	[B]	2l	744g	£9600	
Violation of ceorl's protection	[B]	6s	46g	£600	
Violation of church protection	[B]	50s	387g	£5000	
Violation of the king's protection	[B]	5l	1860g	£24,000	

There were many other fines, but including them all would take up too much space. What is clear, though, is that in Anglo-Saxon England what was most important was not what you did, but who you did it to.

Weregilds

Ceorl	[B]	200s	1550g	£20,000	
King's Welsh Horseman	[B]	200s	1550g	£20,000	
Landed Welsh	[B]	80s	620g	£8000	with ½ Hide
Landless Thegn	[B]	600s	4650g	£60,000	
Landless Welsh	[B]	50s	387g	£5000	
Slave	[B]	60s	465g	£6000	
Thegn	[B]	1200s	9300g	£120,000	
Welsh tribute payer (1 hide)	[B]	120s	930g	£12,000	
Welsh tribute payer's son	[B]	80s	620g	£8000	
Welsh with 5 hides	[B]	600s	4650g	£60,000	

Other

1kg Corn	[W]	2d	3g	£40
Beaver Skin	[B]	120d	186d	£2400
Bridle	[W]	6.5d	10g	£130
Buckle	[W]	3.25d	5g	£65
Cloak	[N]	7.75d	12g	£155
Cow eye	[B]	1d	1.5g	£20
Cow horn	[B]	2d	3g	£40
Cow Tail	[B]	5d	8g	£100
Fleece	[B]	2d	3g	£40
Fox skin	[B]	8d	12g	£160
Fyrdsman's pay/month	[B]	10s	77g	£1000
Hide of land	[B]	1l	372g	£4800
Knife	[W]	2d	3g	£40
Land tax/hide	[B]	2s	15g	£200
Marten Skin	[B]	24d	37g	£480
Otter skin	[B]	8d	12g	£160
Ox Eye	[B]	5d	8g	£100
Ox Horn	[B]	10d	15g	£200
Ox Tail	[B]	1s	8g	£100
Silk (1oz)	[E]	37d	57g	£740
Spurs	[W]	13d	20g	£400
Stirrups	[W]	81.25d	126g	£1625
Wolf skin	[B]	8d	12g	£160

This chapter is derived in part from an article by Ben Levick originally printed in the house journal of Regia Anglorum.

I am delighted to have this opportunity of crediting his original research.

10 Ship

Across the bright sea came the good ship
Bounding along with a bone in her teeth.
And good cheer hovered on many a lip —
Iron-hard cloth and oaken beneath.

Lt Jon Taylor RN. (1806)

A discussion of shipbuilding techniques in a work about weapons might seem somewhat out of place. However, the use of tools to work in hardwoods certainly placed heavy day-to-day demands upon iron that was reflected in better metal finishing and tool and weapon construction. Further, it gives an important insight into the level of commitment and effort that went into building these ships, both for the rich aristocrats that funded most of the big Drakkars — or warships — down to the smaller fjord raiders used for settling more local scores. It is hard to quantify the expense of building a Drakkar in today's terms because the ratio of silver to labour and materials has changed so dramatically over the centuries. A parallel might be that of a wealthy man buying a private jet plane, such as a Lear, today, with building them in quantity being a matter for the State. Towards the end of the Viking Age, suitable trees for the construction of the really big warships were becoming hard to find and this would certainly have driven the price of oak very high.

Without their ships there would have been no Viking Age. But like so many truisms, it is not as simple as that. We might also say that the vessels the Norse folk used to 'see the land of strangers, far away' were just a stage in the Northern development of the ocean-going ship. It is, after all, these hulls that have captured our imagination — but it is only a small part of this story. Within the last 25 years we have discovered wrecks and other fragmentary survivals that have changed our entire outlook on the ships and boats in use at this time.

The use to which these seafaring people put them placed demands upon their vessels which were addressed by changing and developing the design. It is far more widely

49 Most ships sailing out of Scandinavia had peaceful intent

appreciated these days that there was more than one style of 'Viking Ship'. The Northern European style of open-hulled vessel had evolved as far as it could by the end of the period. The Bremen Cog is certainly a development of the earlier type of ship, but it incorporated features that set it aside from the earlier hulls.

One can perhaps draw an engineering parallel between the Viking Drakkar at the end of the eleventh century and the low-wing, monoplane, propeller-driven fighter at the end of the Second World War. Each of the main combatant states were producing variants of the same style of aircraft and without radical change (like developing the sealed deck in the one case and the jet engine in the other) this style of ship and aircraft had reached the limits of its design capability.

It is possible to trace a line of constructional techniques that lead directly from dugout canoe to the great Drakkars. Once the construction moved away from the log boat principal, they evolved quite swiftly, although it took centuries of random development until at last the little fishing boats used for crossing the fjord were capable of crossing the North Sea. But there were areas of divergence, form following function. The shallow-draft almost keel-less hulls used close inshore and in rivers and lakes became so lightly built they could be dragged out of the water and repeatedly pulled from one river to another, allowing traders to travel great distances east from the Baltic into Western Russia and beyond.

All these things are true. The narrow and predatory raiders, big enough to carry a large crew and capable of crossing the North Sea under oars if need be were a far cry from the heavy deep-sea traders that carried Erik the Red to Iceland and Greenland and his son Leif to America. And no one in his right mind would have taken a lightweight river trader — its woodwork lightened to within an inch of its life — far offshore. After all, you might use a Mini to go to the shops, but if you want to stock a supermarket, you need a 40-tonne articulated lorry. That said, these vessels had a lot of things in common and it is interesting to trace the development line.

Take a tree trunk and hollow it out, arriving at the shape we all know from childhood — the log boat or dugout. I've been personally involved in building a couple of these and it is a week's work with hand tools for a crew of fit young men to arrive at something light enough to float with a paddler on board. The word 'unstable' really doesn't do it justice and it will fall over extremely easily. Add a passenger and all your freeboard vanishes, the smallest wave lapping water into the shallow hull. One can only paddle with the greatest care and casting nets etc. requires a degree of balance and ability that is not swiftly learned.

The next stage is to take more advantage of the wood you've got and by strongly binding the ends of the log to stop them splitting out, it is possible to cut a narrow slot in the top of the log and hollow out the trunk from there. Next, you light a long, slow fire inside the tree trunk. The plot is to make the green wood very hot indeed, thus making it even more malleable than it is already. Wedging out the top of the slot uncurves the tree, thus spreading the wood out and making the dugout higher sided. The tension tends to pull the ends up too, which is very handy in anything used at sea. It cannot have been long before the owners of the simplest (and now old-fashioned) types had the idea of splitting out a couple of planks from another log and sewing them onto the top of the log boat with larch roots, thus arriving at the same result for less trouble.

50 The carving from Bro in Gotland, Denmark

The result of this was a boat that was high enough sided to carry useful loads, but was still desperately unstable as it was so narrow. Along comes a man with another, thicker plank and, splitting the log boat right down the middle, inserts the plank into the bottom to widen the hull. One can imagine the consternation of the boat-builder as someone rips his expensive boat apart and fits the plank. However I imagine it would take about 30 seconds manoeuvering in the water to come to the conclusion that he was absolutely right and the log boat was very much more use than it was before.

This development didn't happen overnight and some of it is supposition, but what little evidence we have certainly points in the direction of this line of development. From log boat through to the strange looking Hrotsprung Boat to the Ladby Boat and beyond one can trace the thread of thought and experiment that made the great 'Viking Age' a viable possibility.

All ships at this time were principally made of wood. For most ships, oak was the preferred timber. However ash, elm, pine, larch and several other woods were used at one time or another. The only exception seems to have been warships and for these oak was used exclusively — and was always iron-riveted too. It may be that the use of oak and iron had a ritual pagan significance in this context, both oak and iron being associated with the Odinistic cult. These considerations aside, the wood is well chosen, being a strong, tough timber and well suited to a hull that remains immersed in water, but it will not take being hauled out of the water for very long. Whilst it is well soaked in salt water and painted regularly with pitch, it will last for decades. The keel for Nelson's *Victory* was laid in 1759 and she was in service from 1765, making her nearly 50 years old when she stood in the battle line at Trafalgar in 1805. Oak used in this way gets harder and laden with salt — but if it dries out properly, it will twist and crack, causing permanent shakes that will weaken the hull beyond further use at sea. If you have seen the *Odin's Raven* ship replica in the Peel Viking Centre in the Isle of Man, you might have noticed that it is riven with shakes from stem to stern, a sad end for a vessel built in the late 1970s and not yet out of its infancy.

Other woods fare better in this respect. Larch is pretty good for instance and a half-scale Gokstad ship replica in larch once owned by the *Regia Anglorum* re-enactment society was in and out of the water for seven years, sometimes spending months in one state or the other. Although there were shakes that opened and closed with the humidity, the hull was still capable of tightening up within a day or so of being immersed. The worst of the splits appeared where the wood was under the greatest tension at bow and stern, and most of these were above the waterline. Originally built for the feature film *Erik the Viking*, this replica may still be seen as a permanent feature in the Valhalla ride at Blackpool Pleasure beach, a fittingly showbizzy conclusion perhaps. Another vessel owned by this society is a 19ft (5.8m) long replica of the Gokstad Faering, a four-oared boat. Being small and easily trailered, it is hauled to and fro across the country and is constantly in and out of both salt water and fresh. This hull was also made of larch, a timber described once to the author as a hard softwood! After some four years of this abuse, it began to show a few signs of leaking, easily cured by sealing the joints between the strakes. It might be worth mentioning that this little boat had no sealing compound between the strake edges, relying completely on good edge contact for its waterproof qualities.

The northern shipwrights also reused old planks, incorporating them in other hulls, sometimes by way of a repair or to eke out available timber in new hulls. The best-known example of this is probably a plank from one of the Skuldelev wrecks which had oar ports cut on it that had been carefully patched. It also had new ones cut in it elsewhere. The Skuldelev wrecks also showed that wood from various different species of tree might be used in building or repairing one hull. Its amazing what you can cover up with a nice coat of thick black gungy pitch — as many a second-hand car dealer knows. Of course, we can then readily deduce that new planks were expensive enough to make it worthwhile going to all the trouble of carefully filing off the rivet heads and knocking out the nails without splitting the wood. As someone who has tried it, I can tell you that to manage this with each rivet in a line perhaps less than an inch from the edge of the plank is no mean achievement. Therefore, one might also deduce that this was not a job you gave to the fellow who swept up the chippings. It is worthwhile noting that this recycling of planks is unlikely to be a by-product of recovering the iron from the nails. This can be as well achieved by setting old ships on fire and collecting the iron from the ashes.

The Norse shipwrights fully understood the differing requirements of the hull needed to cross the open sea or be hauled repeatedly across portages. Their job would include choosing the tree as it grew in the forest and I've no doubt at all that those who were best at this were at a premium. These specialists could look at a tree in winter and accurately assess just which trees were best for the various complicated tasks the wood had to do when it was cut to shape and fitted into a ship.

Different parts of the ship came from different parts of the tree and you can see some elements shown in white in the graphics on p.109. They took advantage of naturally grown 'joints' where branches grew from the main trunk. These are stronger than any man-made woodworking joint, and avoid the need for glue or clenched nails in the construction. Such timber also has the advantage that parts made from naturally grown curves are far more resistant to twisting and splitting than ordinary straight-grown wood that has been cut to shape.

There were always ships requiring attention, maintenance and modifications, keeping the shipwrights busy in between new commissions. Only the king and some of the more powerful chieftains would commission new large war or trading vessels, paid for either by taxes or by obligations because of national security. The smaller fishing boats, coastal traders etc. were within the means of the lower social classes. However, we do not know whether there was a system of credit to cover the cost of construction which was then repaid in some shape or form. Log boats, although a very archaic style of boat, were still quite common as they are easy to make, and cheap. If you were only needed to cross small rivers or lakes, or even move a few livestock, then a log boat would suffice. The log boat was such a durable design, that its construction lasted until the early eighteenth century in England, and was still being made in places such as Poland in the 1930s.

Before anything was constructed the tree had to be cut down. This would be done with axes and wedges. The trunk was notched in the direction you wanted it to fall. Then a deep cut was made on the opposite side and wedges driven in to help push the tree over. The limbs and branches that met the trunk were cut free before the tree was felled, to prevent them from being shattered by the weight of the tree as it fell. This of course could only be done with the smaller components involving the outer limbs.

There is some equipment found that has been identified as tree-climbing tackle, so that the worker could ascend the tree in a seat/sling. From there he might support a particular branch with lines to assistants on the ground. The tree branch would then be cut free, and lowered carefully to the floor.

Almost all of the carpentry work would have been done with axes and adzes of various kinds — an adze being an axe with the blade turned through 90 degrees. Hammers, wedges, chisels, drawknives and planes were also in common use and any modern woodworker would readily recognise and be able to use the tools from a Norse shipwright's tool chest. Bow drills with spoon bits were also known and burning irons were sometimes used for the making of holes. The one tool that would have been uncommon was saws, although most types were known and in use.

Before we move on from tools, some attention must be paid to one tool in particular: a wood working plane in the Maidstone Museum in Kent. Of Saxon origin and dated to about AD 600, it is made of a bronze foot plate with an iron blade and the stock is of antler. The real surprise is the size, as the blade cannot be more than half an inch across. This is a cabinetmaker's tool and was in use over 200 years before the Viking Age even began.

Trees were probably felled after the fall of leaf in the autumn and November is the best time. The felled trunk and main branches would be carefully stacked in the open air in piles that allowed the air to circulate close to an open-sided ship house. This was simply a roof supported on corner posts without walls. This stopped precipitation from falling on you and the ship whilst allowing the humidity to remain substantially the same as outdoors. Ships were usually built over winter, the wood being worked green. In winter, unseasoned timber is a lot more stable than at other times of year as the naturally low temperature helps to maintain the woods humidity. This is particularly important with oak as the wood is much easier to work when it is in this state. Once it has dried it might be more stable, but it is a great deal harder to work and bend. Sometimes, wood would be sunk in a bog or into the edge of the fjord or river, thus maintaining its flexibility.

51 The keelson as planned on an idealised tree trunk

52 Components to be selected from another oak tree

53 Peeling with a bark spade

Once the tree was down, the bits that were not going to be used would be trimmed off. Almost nothing of the tree would be wasted. Oak bark went to tan hides and skins; the bast fibres just beneath the bark were used to make rope; the twigs were chopped up and added to sawdust and chippings and used to smoke fish, meat and cheese; and the smaller off-cuts saved to make charcoal. The main part of the trunk would then be split into wedge-shaped sections like slices of cake (as seen in cross-section) and these slices were then trimmed into planks. This was done by shaving off part of one of the sides, and then shaving off some of the thinnest edge to make a flat plank.

Although there were iron saws in existence to help with this kind of work, they were not common, as the blades were particularly difficult to forge. In the Domesday book, compiled in AD 1086, there is mention of only 13 saws in England at the time of Edward the Confessor. It is probable that these were big pit saws that could be used to separate a

54 Logs are split rather than cut, as the split always follows the grain and doesn't cut across it

plank from a log by sawing. The name gives the use, the trunk being laid along the length of the pit, one man standing on the log, the other in the pit.

Splitting a log involves starting a split with an axe, and whilst the axe is still lodged in the timber, an oak wedge is then hammered into the split next to the axehead. The axe can then be hammered in further with a wooden mallet. This will make the split travel down the length of the log. Another wedge is added, and the first is banged further in. The axe can then be removed and sometimes hammered in further along the split. So the process goes on, with most of the work being done by the wedges and saving the precious axehead.

55 Squared logs rebated to go over ribs in the ship

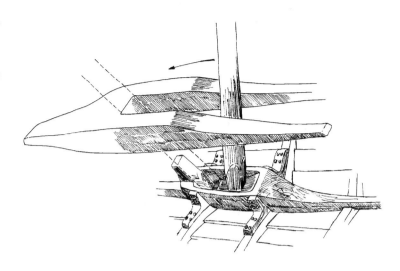

56 The older style ships used very heavy timbers as here with the keelson and mast fish to anchor the mast in the first place

The split can be controlled to some extent, but a good carpenter would select a tree that hadn't twisted as it had grown over the years. A prevailing wind is the culprit here, forcing the tree to withstand the forces of the wind direction and grow stouter on one side.

Trees grown in woods and forests naturally tend to grow straighter, partly because they have to compete for light and space and are not gnarled and twisted anywhere nearly as badly as 'open field' trees that do not have any neighbours to shelter behind. Conversely, an open field oak would be more likely to produce ribs, knees and other shaped pieces. When making planks by splitting the timber in this way, the carpenter is working *with* the wood so as to get the greatest strength out of it. A saw just cuts through the grain instead of following it.

A large log may not be turned into planks, the shipwright might leave half of the tree unsplit for bigger parts of the ship like the keel, ribs or the mast step. In **56**, you can see the mast step, which was sometimes called the keelson, 'The Crone' or even 'The Old Woman'. Made from a solid piece of heavy timber, it accepts the stump end of the mast on top of the keel and bridges several ribs. One can easily see the sexual connotation in this and there seems no doubt that this is where the curious name comes from. It is principally responsible for transmitting the thrust from the sail to the hull. It must take the weight of the mast and not allow it to nod to and fro or from side to side. This was a place where a shaped piece of naturally grown timber would be used. Taking a part of the trunk where a branch grew from it, a groove is hollowed out, leaving the stump end of the branch to act as a support for the mast forward of centre.

The mast is slotted into place in the keelson and sits inside the mast partner or 'The Whale' at deck height. This timber seems to have only been used on decked ships (like Gokstad), spreading part of the thrust from the mast through the cross beams to a special strake in the hull which is perceptibly thicker than the rest. Many ships were undecked and here the whale was replaced by a large crossbeam serving as one of the thwarts. In some ships these timbers acted as seats for the rowers. One might even roughly date Norse vessels by the type of mast support that is fitted to the vessel. The bigger keelsons

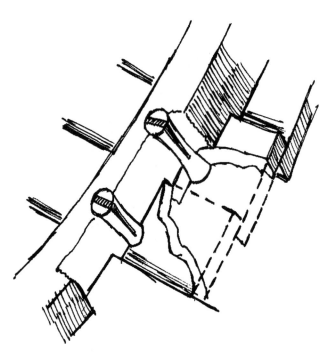

were in use earlier than the less cumbersome method involving the bigger crossbeam roughly at the mid-point of the ship.

The rest of the support for the Mast came from the lines or Stays that ran from its apex to various anchor points in the ship. We have little evidence for rigging on ships constructed in the Northern tradition during the Viking Age. However, from a freehand sketch on a rib bone from Bergen, which has survived, from common sense and later traditions, it is possible to make a sensible stab at what the standing and running rigging would have required. They seem to have preferred two side stays per side set a little aft of the mast to act as a support from the mast under sail, rather than a single, larger backstay. There must have been a reason for this that is now lost to us and it is possible that a backstay tended to pull the sternpost upwards and forwards, thus making the hull 'work' at the sternpost. This would make it leak at best and tear the ship apart at worst — but it must be stressed that this is a supposition being advanced, not something proven by experiment.

To start with, ships were made without joins in the strakes and the Nydam ship is made from a very few very long wide planks. However, they very soon learned to scarf butt ends together, thus saving a great deal of timber. Still, they had some curious ideas and — for instance — would laboriously adze a plank flat, leaving several lumps proud of the surface. When the plank was finished, these lugs would be drilled through and the ribs tied to them. The Gokstad ship was made like this and she was built around AD 900. Later on, shipbuilders found that they could make the lugs separately and rivet them on after the hull was built, thus saving hundreds of hours of hard work and practically halving the amount of timber required to make a ship.

*58 An example of strakes lashed with
bast fibre ropes to the ribs*

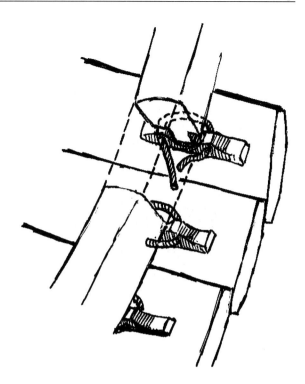

Sometimes parts would be held together with trenails, wooden pins that were split and wedged to hold them in place. As iron was as expensive in those days as silver is to us today, trenails, which are 'wooden rivets', might be employed in many areas of the hull, usually when the joint was in tension rather than sheer. They are simply wooden dowels that are driven into previously bored holes through the component pieces. However, making round wooden pegs of a consistent size and taper on a pole lathe is no easy matter. The teenail must be a fairly hard drive fit in its hole, otherwise it will not lock properly (**57**). Yet it must not be too big or it will swell when it gets wet and could easily split the plank. When driven into the hole prepared for it by drilling or burning, a small split is started into which a little wedge is driven. Sometimes, the trenail was not blind ended and this is repeated at the other end. This locks the trenail in place, neither being able to work it's way forward or back. There is some research that has shown that if the parts of the 'nail' are boiled in linseed oil prior to being assembled, they will remain locked together almost indefinitely. Another advantage of this would be to stop the trenail absorbing water, thus stopping it from swelling or rotting. The Slavic tradition of Viking ship building such as from Northern Poland owes a lot to the trenail, and less to the use of iron. In the western half of the Viking world, it was the other way round.

It was commonplace for the ribs to be lashed in place with bast fibre cords that had been soaked in pitch to preserve them. The cord is sewn through the ribs and the strakes, with special cleats left on the planks for the job. It is was a very time-consuming task to make a hull in this way, but it did save on expensive iron nails. Although it may seem odd to the uninitiated, these hulls were built from the skin inwards. After the strakes were in

59 One of the shipwright's team uses an adze to shape a sternpost

place, the ribs would be tied in, their purpose principally being to offer support for the internal timbers. This is one of the very real differences that separates ships built in the Viking tradition from those influenced by Mediterranean vessels. Following on the Roman original, these were built from the inside out and have heavy ribs that support the hull to which they are rigidly attached. Clinker-built ships with loosely attached ribs can be very lightly built for their size, enabling the hull to twist in the water. This absorbs the twisting force imparted by the wave energy without over-stressing the hull. It is impossible to build a sealed deck on such a vessel, so until the hull was made a lot more rigid, seafarers were going to sea in open-topped water tanks. It can be no coincidence that almost every longship replica I have ever sailed in had at least one man bailing most of the time.

Whatever wood the shipbuilder decided to make the hull from, the keel and its endpost extensions were invariably made of oak. On most later ships, the bowpost and sternpost were specially shaped to accept the ends of the strakes or planks that formed the hull of the ship. This was because the shaping of the plank ends to fit an unshaped end post was very expensive in timber, and you could get a better watertight joint with the larger sealing area provided by a shaped post. The distortion of the midship planks as they rose at their ends in addition to the inward tapering and narrowing ends of the strakes created the upward curving nature of the Viking hulls. This became stylised and hulls like that of the Oseberg ship with its broad, sweeping bow and stern are not as seaworthy as the later less pronounced styles. I have seen a half-scale replica of this type which had less than nine inches of freeboard. Oseberg has three strakes added for most of its length and I have a sneaking suspicion that this was done immediately after launch during which it sank.

It is the style of construction that was essentially the cause of the Viking ship's outline. Had they followed other techniques in building, the Viking ship as we now picture it would not have happened. An interesting diversion from the Viking style of ship construction can be seen at the museum of Utrecht. This type of hull is called a Hulk construction, giving the ship a banana-shaped hull which has low prows. It can also be seen stamped as a symbol onto coins from the area, which first alerted historians as to the uniqueness of this style of construction.

Major components like bow and sternpost were sometimes manufactured in advance of the rest of the vessel and stored in bogs (perhaps to stabilise the green timber), as a find from Scotland attests. Archaeologists are stumped to come up with any other answer than the work had to come to a halt for some reason and the posts were stored in the water to prevent them from drying out prior to continued work at another time. It indicates too that these shipwrights possibly knew the value of storing oak in an acidic peat bog rather than a lake or river.

The sternpost was a very large piece of wood and — as in later wooden vessels too — governed the final height of the finished ship's bow and stern. This in turn dictated the length of the ship, so trees big enough to make these special posts would have been very valuable. Taking several hundred years to attain the great size necessary, by the end of the Viking Age it was becoming more and more problematic to find trees in Scandinavia big enough to provide really heavy timbers.

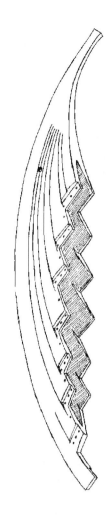

60 A completed oak sternpost

Shipbuilders were forced to seek far and wide for these timbers, and to begin considering different building practices.

Once the main timbers had been chosen and carved from the solid wood, the construction of the hull of the ship could begin. The keel was the lowest, central and the most important timber in the ship. It ran from one end to the other as a single piece of wood, with the bowpost and sternpost being attached at either end. It would be constructed lying the correct way up in situ near the riverside. The posts and the keel would then be joined with iron nails, the three main sections forming a whole upon which a ship was based that might have a life of nearly a hundred years. Keel and endposts were

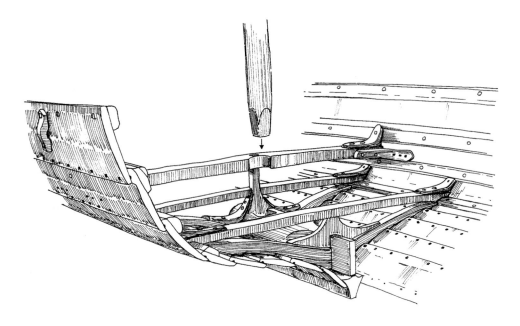

61 In the later style ships, reliance on huge timbers to support the mast was replaced by rigging and lateral struts

then firmly wedged upright with rocks and wooden props.

The first of the strakes would then be shaped and clamped in place, holes drilled through both pieces of wood and iron nails driven in hold the garboard strake into place. This garboard strake is one of the trickiest components to fit, as it is in practice a flexible plank joined to a fairly inflexible keel. There is always the tendency for the ship to leak at this point. To counter this, animal hair rolled in hot pitch (made ideally by roasting birch roots to obtain the hot sap) was trapped between the edges of the joint. There can be few task invented by man that are more filthy to carry out than hot caulking a clinker built ship.

All Viking ships (and all ships in northern Europe for centuries before and after the Viking Age) were made by this method of overlapping the edges of the strakes and riveting the overlap section together. It is called clinker building and makes hulls that are light and pliant: hulls that will flex and bend in the open sea without breaking or letting in too much water. In figure (**62**), the shipwright can be seen clamping two strakes together before roving together. The heads of the iron nails on the joints that he has finished are plainly visible. About 1575lb (700kg) of these iron nails were needed to make a 50ft (15.5m) deep-sea trader and you'll recall that, in round about terms, iron was as expensive as silver is to us today.

After the long wedge of tree has been split off the log, it is smoothed with an axe called a sideaxe. It has a specially designed off-centre blade and a bent handle so that the builder's hands are clear of the work. It does the bulk of the work that one might use a plane for today. One can still be seen in use on the Bayeux Tapestry, and traditional shipwrights still

62 *Another strake is wedged in place ready to be permanently roved onto the emerging ship*

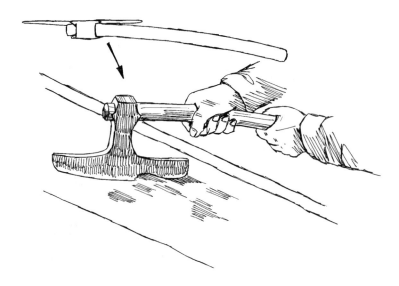

63 The sideaxe is used to flatten and smooth planks split from logs. It has an offset blade and a 'bent' handle to keep the user's hands clear of the work

64 A finished cabe overlaid on the other half of timber that it was carved from

employ this useful tool today.

A ship's plank was not flat in section. It had a sloping top edge with a groove cut in the lower edge for the caulking of pitched animal hair. The top and bottom were not straight, but cut to follow the line of the hull in any particular place. Once the strake had been shaped, then it was clamped into place on the hull, and then riveted home. It is important to note that the nail is driven through a hole that has already been drilled through the strake. If this is not done the wood will almost always split, if not when you are riveting the pieces together, then later — perhaps miles from land.

After the nail has been driven through, then a special washer called a rove is forced hard over it, actually recessing into the wood a little way. The nail is square in section and the rove has a round hole punched in the centre, thus ensuring a good fit. The end of the nail is trimmed to size and then beaten with a hammer to make it too big to go back through the hole and this riveted nail cannot move again without snapping off.

As each strake is added, and the ship begins to take shape, only then are some of the

65 A sideaxe in use. The strake is wedged upright so that the axe can be used in the vertical plane

ribs anchored into place. This can be considered as building the boat back-to-front. More recent 'traditional' shipbuilding methods involve constructing the frames first on the keel and then adding the strakes after. This method cannot be used on a Viking-style hull, as the ribs are only tied to cleats in the hull and do not impart sufficient additional stiffness to be used in the same way as ribs in a 'frame-first' hull. In addition, a hull of this latter type requires accurate plans so that opposing ribs are identical. 'Odin's Raven' was built almost entirely without plans — although I understand that the builders had some to hand before construction was completed.

As far as we can tell, it was the Vikings that invented and refined this method of constructing ships and boats and it certainly allows you to make open hulls of great flexibility. However, it is not practical to seal the deck to such a flexible hull and therefore it was never possible to build a ship like this which did not act as a huge water tank in the rain or in breaking seas. The necessity of such a design meant that they either sailed only on the finest days in light breezes, or the mariners a thousand years ago were very hardy. The Sagas attest to their courage at sea in all conditions, and it would be ridiculous to think that they could avoid all poor weather, all of which warrants our great respect. One area of investigation that has yet to be looked into in any detail is the clothes that they wore

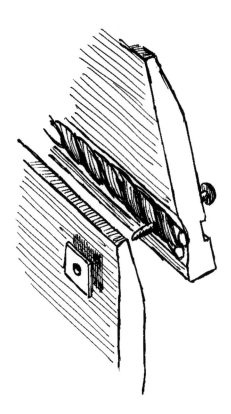

66 *An example of roving. You can also make out the complex cross-section of the strake*

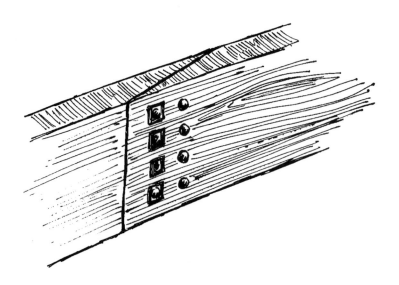

67 *A scarf joint roved through from either side*

specifically for sailing. Once wet, hypothermia will set in
very quickly causing death quite rapidly. They must have
been aware of the consequences, even if they did not
understand the process. The author can bear witness as
to how uncomfortable it can be once you are cold to the
core and well off the shore in a stiffer wind than was
expected. There is precious little shelter in a Longship.

Usually, planks are too short for a complete strake,
especially on a large vessel, so they are joined together
with a scarf joint (**67**). The planks have to be drilled and
riveted together side by side with a diagonal chamfer at
their ends.

Masts were hewn from straight growing pine or fir
trees and little shaping was required. The timber is
naturally flexible and could be replaced at need as it was
not fixed permanently to the hull. To top of the mast
would necessarily carry the fittings for the various ropes
that were fixed to it, but here we can only use common
sense speculation as none have ever been discovered.

Steering oars came in various shapes and it seems to
have been a matter of personal taste as to which one you
used. The use of the side-rudder was the one great flaw
of Viking Age ship design as it imposes considerable
restrictions and considerations as to how the ships can
be handled. The steering oar (or rudder) fits over a solid
rounded piece of wood attached to the hull, usually
referred to as the 'tit', for the sound reason that it bears
a striking resemblance to a female breast. The blade
pivots on the tit and the rudder is roped through the hull
and the tit with woven larch root cord which is then
tightened up to draw the rudder tight into the hull. They
always give trouble and it is really hard to see how the

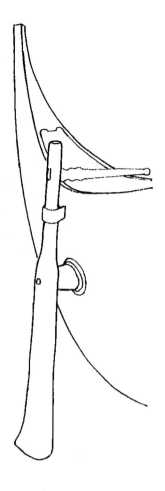

*68 The usual layout of the tiller
and rudder*

Viking made them work as well as they apparently did. There were spares below the
steering step on the Gokstad ship, so they must have expected that there would be
continuing problems with this item through this world and into the next.

The rudder is also secured with a heavy leather strap to stop it flapping about and a
rope from the top of the shaft runs back past the samson post to the last rib. This is done
to stop the water drag from pulling the rudder forward when the ship is running at speed.
Anything above 4-5 knots makes it difficult to keep hold of the rudder bar, particularly if
there is a cross-sea running. In addition to all these elements, the rudder also has a line
running from its lower tip to help raise the rudder when the ship is in shallow water or
about to beach. Failure to haul it up in time especially if the ship is aback, something
which is very common in a hull with no transom, will ensure that the mass of the ship will
tear it free in a trice when it strikes anything immovable such as land. The ship can be

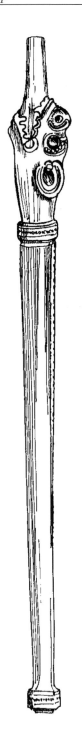

easily steered with the oars doing all the work when the sail is down. The carved steering handle is worth noting, decorated by a people who loved complex art.

At different parts of the hull, the shipwright would use different methods of holding the ribs of the ship in place. These were always fitted to these vessels after the hull was built and previous graphics show them tied in with larch roots or sometimes trenailed into place. All of the ribs and other components known as knees were cut from the curved parts of the trees where a branch met the trunk. From any one joint like this on the tree, at least two opposing knees can be split from the join. The grain is not compromised, or cut through thereby making it weak, resulting in a very strong part for the ship.

An uncomplicated example of this use of wood can be seen on smaller boats. The cabes, known today as rowlocks, were carved out of a single piece of wood at the point where a branch left the tree trunk. The fork of the branch acts as the backstop for the oar. The small hole through the cabe takes a rope which loops around the oar keeping it up against the cabe. Today, in wood, shipwrights would use a pre-bent and shaped laminate to achieve the same end. At the ends of some of the cross members that brace the ship's hull laterally, three of these knees are used to help support the cross member and keep it in place.

One of the most prominent parts of the Viking ship of our tradition would be its figurehead. These are things of great romance and lore. Whilst it is fairly certain that they did indeed have figureheads on their ships, only a small elite would have carried them, and they would have all been warships of some description. It seems to be the case that the ship head would be stored below deck and only fixed into position before landing on a hostile shore.

There is better evidence for spirals or sunwheels on the sternpost. *Odin's Raven,* the two-thirds Gokstad replica that was built at Odd's yard on Oslo Fjord and sailed to the Isle of Man for its millennium year at the end of the 1970s, had such a device on the sternpost. Firmly based upon the surviving ornament from the Ile de Goix burnt ship burial, this device was found actually to have a purpose. During a somewhat stalwart race between *Odin's Raven* and some nineteenth-century fishing vessels built in the Viking tradition called femborings, one of the latter ranged up to windward. As it came within biscuit toss, its bigger sail took the wind out of the sail of the smaller *Odin's Raven.* As the *Raven* slowed, the relative speed increased and for a moment it looked as thought there was a possibility of being boarded. However, as

69 The tiller from the Oseberg ship

the bowpost came abaft the mast of the *Raven*, the femboring's sail caught on the sharp points of the stern ornament, ripping the cloth from headrope to footrope, spilling the wind and slowing the ship. Interestingly enough, the best place to store spears aboard a small warship is leaning up against the sternpost.

Only the Oseberg ship burial find from southern Norway had any hint of a decorated prow, and these were simply carved spirals, rather than the fearsome dragon heads that we expect. The Gokstad ship, Ladby ship and the Skudulev ships have all survived without any sign of figureheads or a means of fitting one. This can be said of many other period ship finds. So where do we get this idea that they carried them? The simple answer is that the Icelandic Sagas are rife with reference to them and we have little else to go on.

Personally, I rather suspect that they did mount heads on their ships. However, it must be said that the two most regularly quoted and depicted images of figureheads are either not from the Viking period, or are not figureheads. The first to be dealt with is from the River Scheldt in Belgium, and can be found in the British Museum. It is arguable whether this is actually a figurehead of a ship. Exquisitely carved, it is securely dated to the sixth century AD. It is not Viking at all, but possibly early Saxon or Frisian from the same date. The ship head you see in the line drawing (**72**) is based upon a bronze pin found at Hedeby.

The second piece is from the Oseberg find itself. It is often referred to as the piece carved by the 'Academician', because of the intricacy of the work and the restraint shown in not carving every available surface as was commonly the custom. It is a delightful piece of Viking carving, but is too small to be a ship head, and was probably a seat finial or pillar.

Until a ship is excavated with one of these figureheads in position, then the argument will continue. I believe that the sagas are correct in this particular detail, even if they were not the norm. One reference states that ships were obliged to remove their 'heads' prior to entering a foreign port as a sign of their peaceful intentions and it is this peripheral and rather circumstantial evidence that gives ship heads credence.

There have been a few finds of non-ferrous metal weathervanes which seem to be from later period ships, a number of original examples of ships' bronze weathervanes

70 A Viking Age rudder, showing its slender cross-section and the various anchor points, trailing line to raise it, and where the tiller bar was slotted in

71 *The detailed arrangement of the rudder complete with its strops and wedges*

surviving. They seem to have replaced the dragon heads as a more practical option. A scratchwork graffiti bone rib from Bergen gives us some correlation between the finds and their use as it shows a number of ships at anchor with all their 'ends' up against the jetty.

The term 'ends' has been used because it has been said that these weathervanes are on the prows, but this will not stand up to logical argument. When conning one of these vessels, it is frequently impossible to see the bowpost at all because the sail is in the way. Even if you relied upon a third party to tell you what the vane was doing, it would be useless. When the wind spills around the sail, there is a considerable rotor component forward of the mast, giving false readings from a vane so placed. The other possible site for the weathervane could have been the top of the mast. Most of the time the man at the helm would be able to see the vane, but there is some turbulence here too. For a 'clean' picture of the wind, it is best to position the vane on the sternpost. It is above the viewer's head and in line with the main thrust centre of the mast. The silk streamers tied into the holes in its trailing edge would flutter immediately over the head of the helmsman. This

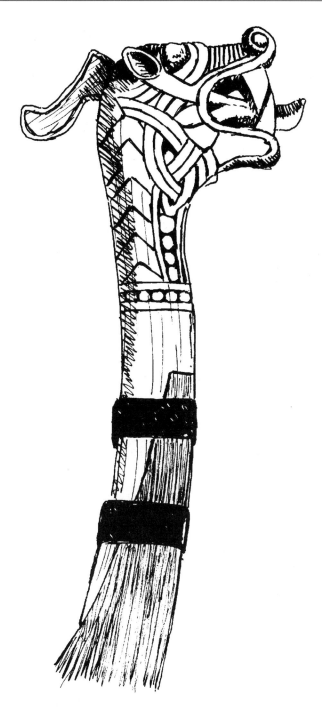

72 *A possible interpretation of a shiphead and a simple means of fitting it to a bowpost*

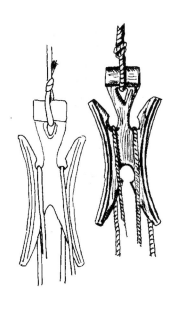

73 Virgins: the Viking's pulley block

would give an audible clue as to the wind's position. I have talked at length with people with experience of side-tillered hulls who tell me that in difficult conditions with the wind aft but gusty, they preferred to face aft whilst steering.

At this point in its construction, the ship would have been approaching completion and would have been time to launch her. It is at this juncture that the 'luck' of the ship was established and much of the Vikings' feeling for this important occasion has come down to us intact across the centuries.

Getting the ship into the water has never been simply a matter of shoving her down the bank into the water. Before the Vikings were Christian, the launching ceremony of a warship involved (we are told) a very bloodthirsty human sacrifice and even today we pour a blood substitute over the bow of a ship when she is launched. Champagne is a very new idea, as it used to be red wine.

With the ship in the water, it is time to step the mast and attend to the rigging. Most ship-rope in the Viking Age was not made of hemp but linen. Some rope-makers used horsehair from horsetails and others — where great strength was required — greased Walrus hide. The latter must have been an extremely smelly product. To be honest, what we know of Viking ship rigging (the ropes and lines which are used to sail the ship) is mostly worked out on a 'it was probably like this' basis as no-one bothered to write it down or draw it out. Ships found in the archaeological record do not tell us much, as all the ropes have rotted away long ago leaving only the wooden parts of the rigging system, and even then it is not remotely complete. So various sources have been amalgamated to form whole sets of rigging for one ship. From what we have found, by experimenting to see how it might have worked, and from more recent Nordic fishing vessels that survived until the Second World War, figure (**75**) shows how some of the rigging that supported one side of the mast to the hull probably looked.

The pulley block had not been invented at this time and the Vikings used curious devices called 'virgins', 'angels' or 'maidens'. They are not a great idea as they often jam and occasionally break. Like the rudder, it is hard to understand how they worked as well as they apparently did. Only from use on voyages recreated today can we be sure that these rigging components do indeed work, even if they can be taxing. The Viking sailors put up with these idiosyncrasies because they knew no better and found life to be quite tolerable despite the absence of the stern rudder and pulley block, decent food and a bed to sleep in.

In a few short centuries, the Norsemen developed the ship in the northern tradition to enable them to rove where they would across the northern seas. The deep-sea traders took them first to the Atlantic Islands above Scotland and on to Iceland, Greenland and

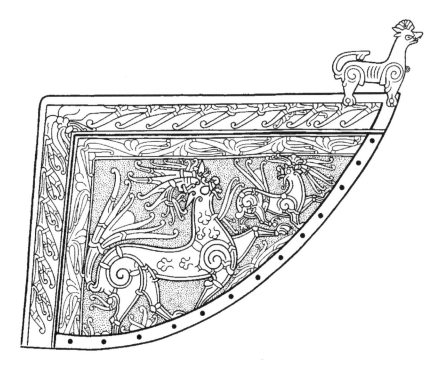

74 *A ships weathervane*

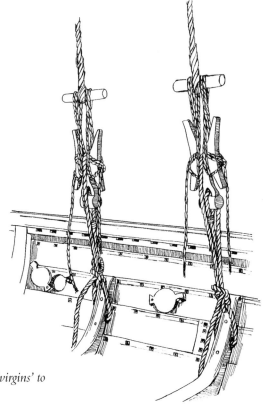

75 *An example of some of the rigging using 'virgins' to help anchor the mast*

76 *Rowing her out, a long hard pull if the tide's against you*

finally to America. Their small craft were mainly used to travel across the fjords and for inshore fishing. The great Drakkars were feared throughout the known world and became synonymous with the age of individual militarism that bridged the years around the turn of the first millennium after Christ.

Yet the days of the Longship were numbered. In the early twelfth century, on the west coast of Europe the cog was being developed. Unlike the Longship, the bowposts and sternposts were vertical, changing the shape of the hull and facilitating the transition to the stern rudder, which must have been a great relief to everyone. The hull became stiffer and the ribs larger, leading to the ability to seal the deck, although we do not know when this was first done.

The earliest known reference to this changeover is to be seen on the font of Winchester Cathedral, constructed *c.*AD 1180. In the thirteenth century, the seal of the port of Winchelsea shows a warship with a high, curved prow and stern complete with forecastle and after castle. The vessel has a side rudder and — unusual for this type of hull — a backstay. There are no oarports indicated at all, something which invites further study.

The seal of Stralsund, done in AD 1329, shows for the first time the cog, complete with stern rudder. The vessel has no backstay but is heavily side-stayed both fore and aft,

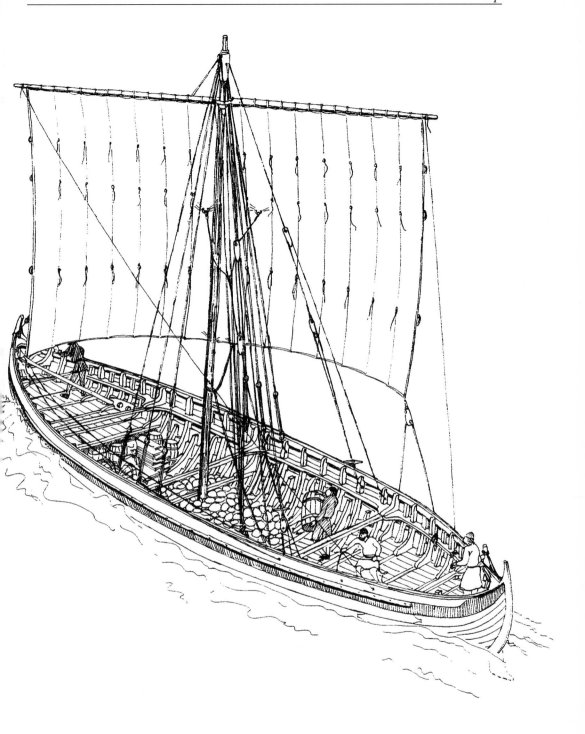

77 A deep sea trader sailing in ballast. No wonder the helmsman's nervous

78 *Longship and Cog. The Skanstrup painting. This painting was done about AD 1400 and can be seen in the church at Skanstrup. It is an excellent contemporary reference showing both of these types of vessels in use at the same time*

the port side stays being omitted for the sake of clarity one assumes. Once again, there are no oarports.

The change over from the open rowing boat that formed the basis for even the most sophisticated Viking ships represented a development that led to stronger and ultimately larger ships. The cog had a stiffness in the hull that could lead to a sealed deck, the next great step forward in ship technology.

79 Stern rudder at Winchester

80 These two ship seals from Winchlesea and Stralsund illustrate the development of the northern ship as the Mediterranean influence started to make inroads into the north

11 Sea

Oft times upon the night watch
My feet were bound in bonds of frost
As the ship beat past the cliffs
Yet my heart's blood stirs me once more to go
Upon the towering seas, the salt waves play
... To see the land of strangers, far away

The Seafarer

Not all Viking ships were great sea-going vessels. A more common sight would have been smaller boats that were used to cross the fjords and rivers. From these, you could ferry a few people from shore to shore, fish, sink fish traps, or move some co-operative livestock to better forage on the opposite bank. This particular boat is called a 'Faering', meaning literally four oars. In modern terms this is called double sculls, where each rower has two oars. The man on the tiller or steerboard is not essential when rowing, as the rowers can steer the boat via the oars. The tiller cannot be lashed into a neutral position so that it does not affect the rowers, however its affect can be avoided when the tiller handle is removed, swivelled clear of the water, and strapped up. It has a useful function though as the steersman takes the problem of directional control from the rowers as he can see ahead more readily. This is a very relaxing position to be in in the boat, although you tend to get cold as you are not exercising your muscles.

The only time things get exciting is when this particular little vessel is sailed. The small boat is very twitchy in the wind as it is an unballasted vessel and any sudden change in the wind direction can throw the boat this way or that. The small tiller has a surprising amount of effect as the speed of the boat picks up, which requires the man on the tiller to have a steady hand. The rowers, who should really only number two not including the

81 River work. Small vessels like this draw less than two feet and can be pursuaded through some remarkably shallow rivers

steersman, then act as 'rope pullers/holders', assisting in the sailing of the boat. There is no anchor, so the Faering has to make for the shore, or tie up to another anchored boat, unless you can rely on not drifting as the crew takes a nap.

The lack of a deep keel and relatively high sides encourages the wind to drift the boat sideways in the water, an effect that all Viking ships suffered to one extent or another, whether under sail or not. This is called giving leeway, i.e. the ship slips sideways into the lee (downwind side) of the wind. This is solely due to the affect of the wind's force on the side of the ship's hull. Critics of Viking ships have described this tendency to skid or slip sideways as 'having as much leeway as a common raft'. Another curiosity of the boat with such an angular keel is that when the nose of such a small boat touches shore, the craft becomes immediately unstable and liable to topple one way or the other flinging the crew into the water at the end of a potentially competent and skilful sail. To prevent a demonstration of forgetfulness, the crew will soberly lower the sail prior to reaching shore and get at least one pair of oars out to steer and organise the boat square on to the shore. If the water is still deep enough to bring the boat side on to the bank of a river (not forgetting that the tiller sits lower in the water than the keel) the crew can then get out easily onto the bank and stay dry.

However, in the sea or in most lakes, the crew will get wet feet and legs as they jump out, which is the better than tipping the crew completely in by accident necessitating the boat to be bailed out. The water comes up to the knees, so that the crew often wear old shoes to protect their feet and take their trousers off to keep them dry for use on shore. On the boat itself, wet leather shoes are a menace. The saturated leather and damp timber cause the crews feet to slip, so some opt to remove their shoes for better grip.

In figure **81** the boat seems to be very cramped, but this is due to some foreshortening in the photograph. Even at 19ft (5.8m) in length, four people are not particularly crowded but this leaves one with precious little freeboard and in choppy conditions you would not want anyone else aboard. In very calm conditions, you can get six or seven people aboard depending upon their total weight and how passive they all are.

The Faering takes six men to lift it clear of the water with a struggle, although it can be pulled along its keel by four far more easily. It's estimated weight is 450lb (200kg), although it has never been accurately weighed. This brings into question the practicality of portage. This is the practice of carrying the boat from one river to a neighbouring one to continue your journey. For economy's sake, and the success of the venture, the crew would be as small as was possible, maximising the volume of goods carried. In this case, a three-man mission would be apt. However, three is too small to move the boat and the cargo. This would suggest that the famous Viking traders on the Russian river systems may have had to employ locals to assist with either horse, ox or manpower to carry the goods, or pull the boat. All of these added to the expenses of the venture and to the eventual price of the goods.

Commissioning, manning and provisioning a warship was something only the very wealthy could afford. They were long, lean and predatory and designed to carry as many warriors as possible for a relatively short distance or time. They carried enough men to change the rowing crew on a fairly regular basis and were not as dependent upon the direction of the wind as the deep-sea cargo vessels. In poor conditions, the warriors might

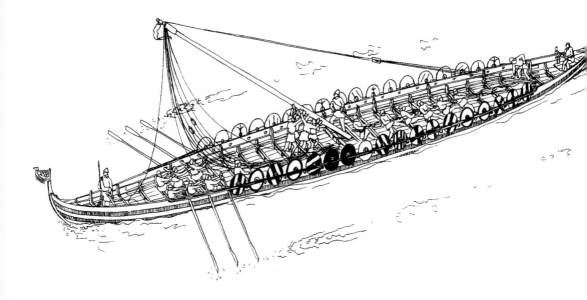

82 Setting up the mast at sea on a big warship would be a dangerous job

hang shields along the side, partly for show and partly for some protection from the driving sea-spray. Whilst they add to the effective freeboard they also expose more surface area to the wind, and using shields at sea in anything but a following wind seems unlikely. The shields found with the Gokstad ship do not appear to have been used in battle and there is a certain simplicity and lightness of construction that leads me to think that they may not have been used in anything except a shipboard context.

Warships were touchy and under-ballasted for speed. As such, they would not have had decks cluttered with gear and cargo so they could be sailed with efficiency and safety. All swords, mail, axes and provisions would be sealed into barrels and stored below deck to try to stop them from rusting in the salt air. The crew would have worn heavy clothing as it is always cold at sea.

It appears that the Vikings set some store in being able to dismount the mast and set it up again. As there were few if any bridges to pass under, it is hard to see why, but certainly all but the largest hulls (or cargo vessels) were capable of having their masts taken down. In anything but a harbour or the calmest of seas, it would have been a hard and fairly dangerous job, particularly without wheel-based pulleys and laid ropes. Further, not all the crew would be available for hauling as some would need to row on until the mast was set and the sail drawing sufficiently to give her good steerage.

Trading vessels like the Skuldelev Wreck One were quite different and capable of long ocean voyages of settlement and exploration. A whole extended family could take ship from Norway to Iceland and carry with it the farm animals, tools and stores that would be needed during the time it took to build a house and settle in before the winter. It is far rounder and deeper in section to contain cargo and might be 50-60ft long (15-18m). The few oars are hardly ever used, with the ship being propelled by just the sail and the skill of the sailors who might be as few as five or six men. Such trading vessels travelled much further and spent longer at sea than the warships, as the trader is a genuine ocean going ship whilst the raider is designed primarily for coastal work and will head for port as soon as conditions get too bad.

The Vikings called this kind of ship 'swan breasted' to describe the bluff, rounded bows that could shoulder aside Atlantic rollers that had gained momentum across 3000 miles of sea. It was rare for one of these hulls to be run ashore. Laden, they drew about 5ft (1.5m) and it was better to offload them by wading the goods ashore or transferring them by smaller craft. The Wreck 1 had almost no scoring on the bottom, but the Wreck 3 from the same find was smaller and lighter and the bottom strakes were much damaged from dragging her up on beaches.

In Gokstad and the Skuldelev Wreck 1, long poles were found that had no apparent use. At deck level and against the inside of the straking, stout blocks were discovered fixed to the hull. Inserting one of these poles into one of the blind holes cut into the blocks, one could fit the other end into a sewn pocket in the bottom corner of the sail. This stretched the cloth well outside the hull in order to change the thrust centre of the sail in an attempt to sail closer to the wind. Alternatively, if it was possible to fit both at once (and it is uncertain whether it is), the sail would gain in performance by having the lower edge of the sail stiffened. This is referred to as 'the beiti-ass method' and it may be from these beiti-ass poles that we get the term 'beating to windward'.

In sailing the ship replica *Black Tern* owned by Regia Anglorum, we found that stretching out one side of the sail in this way with a spare oar did offer a small gain in performance, particularly in light airs. We also experimented with sailing with the wind more or less on the port beam and actually made headway by bringing the yard in line with the hull, hauling the starboard end of the yard down hard right aft and passing the port tack line around the bowpost. This had the effect of bringing the sail so far forward as to virtually change the rig to lateen. The effect was increased by manually handing up the starboard part of the sail to lessen the effect of the wind upon it. I ought to say that we rarely used cleats in sailing this vessel, handing the sheets directly. This meant that we could not get into too much trouble as, if a sudden gust threatened to run away with the ship during trials, you could let the sheet fly before you were whipped overboard. I really could not recommend doing this in anything but a light breeze nor without a number of hardy, strong young men wearing life jackets.

Another method is indicated by finds in relation to the Skuldelev Wreck 3. Small holes were found in the top strake of this vessel and it is possible to reconstruct a different way of spreading out the sail. If an iron pin (a 'seglstikke' or sail stick) is fitted into one of these holes, the tack line can be run around the pin allowing one to haul the sail up hard to increase the performance. To flatten the sail still further, a bowline could run from the leading edge of the sail to the bow post and if the sail is fitted with a number of reinforced eyes, a specially shaped hook called a 'duva hook' can be attached to the sail below the bowline and hauled off on a cleat. This is certainly not recommended in gusty or fluky winds. There are modern parallels for this traditional sailing aid and the principal was in use for centuries in the north.

The Vikings not only looked westward for profit and adventure. They sailed to ports

83 A fluked anchor from the Viking Age

in the Mediterranean. This involved hugging the coasts of Denmark, the Low Countries, France, travelling south to Spain and into the Med. Depending upon the welcome, the ship would have visited some ports to restock supplies and trade some goods. They had to stay overnight at sea sometimes and might light a fire on the ballast. There was no danger of fire with the timbers so soaked in seawater. The real problem lay in the fact that you were unlikely to have any dry wood to burn. An alternative would be to light a fire in a large cauldron that was suspended from a tripod or some element of the rigging, and hang over that a smaller metal pot in which to cook. This would swing with the motion of the boat, so that the pot was always over the fire. Naturally, the ship would be provisioned with dry casks of salted and smoked meats, but the fish helped to stretch the rations. Fish were often hooked, landed, killed, filleted and then spread with small wooden or bone skewers and hung to dry out in the rigging for later use.

Another key reason to visit other ports was to take on fresh water. As the going got hotter as they proceeded south, the crew naturally drank more water. Fresh water was always kept in special barrels that had a lid with a small opening in it, to prevent salt water getting in, and reducing the volume of spillage. On some of the more elaborate versions, the men could drink from a small spout in the top of the cask.

The ports were a good place to clean themselves up too. Despite the traditional image of hairy, smelly Vikings, they combed their hair regularly, washing more often that many

84 *A 'wooden' anchor*
   some 3ft (1m)
   across weighed
   down with the aid
   of a large carved
   rock

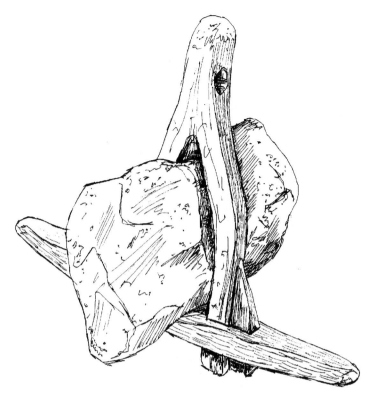

other peoples, even though they did not have the bathtub. Their hair was cut short as well. All of the carvings and imagery that the Vikings left to us demonstrate this. In addition to dressing their hair, they combed and plaited their beards and never let them get too shaggy and straggly.

Crossing the open sea led to navigation and, to be frank, we do not have a clear idea of how these early voyagers found their way around. We know that sometimes they did not and frequently had to cautiously explore strange coastlines to see if the natives were friendly. Even an experienced old hand like Egil Skallagrimsson once found himself cast up on the Yorkshire coast in the country of his great enemy, Erik Bloodaxe. The scent of the sea, tide streams, known currents, dead-reckoning, the movement of sea-birds, the direction of travel and height of the Sun at midday would assist these intrepid navigators. They knew the night sky well and could readily navigate by the stars.

During the day, even when the sun was reclusive, a device similar in some ways to a sundial could have been used to determine position. Sometimes called a sun or shadow compass, it was, in essence, a small disk of wood held horizontally with a handle on the underside. Raised from the centre of the disk was a short gnomon, or pointer that cast a shadow onto the face of the disk. Before one set out on, for example, a voyage to Orkney, the navigator would spend some time in the same latitude as his destination preparing his aid and marking the path of the sun's shadow as it progressed across the disk. When at sea, the shadow was kept as close to the marked track as possible and by matching the shadow

85 On a quiet day at sea, the seafarer sets up his cooking fire on the ballast

and the set marks you could keep on a fairly steady course. This has been checked at sea by none other than the famous yachtsman Robin Knox-Johnson and it did work reasonably well, giving a landfall within ten miles on a hazy day with fitful sun. This however could not take complete account of any drift that was caused by the ship slipping sideways with the wind, nor render an accurate position in cloudy conditions. At this point experience and intuition had to take over — and a certain amount of good luck. I think it is reasonable to draw an analogy between a man on his way to work who travels through heavy traffic without thinking about it. The journey quickly becomes automatic and one navigates just by visual cues learned by familiarity. As an indication of this, the author once knew a fisherman who frequented the Irish Sea off the south-west coast of Wales. If he was below when the boat was heading for home, he could tell where the vessel was by the different sound that the hull made in various parts of the sea. He accounted for the differences mainly by the changes in the reflected sound of the engine, but his grandfather had told him that the same thing occurred under sail for the experienced ear.

The Viking sailors knew their water well and, with no other options to help them, could look at the colour of the sea, the steepness of the waves and the colour of light on the horizon and get a reasonable idea of where they were before they even considered seaweeds, birds and driftwood. For instance, whales gather to feed in some numbers in an area known to be half a day's sailing south of Iceland. A prudent man might carry caged land birds with him and release one each day when he thought he was close to his landfall. With the advantage of height, the bird will be able to see land on the horizon much further away and fly towards it. The seafarer would simply follow it in.

An experienced seafarer may have noticed that the position of the Pole Star in relation to the horizon changed as he moved further south or north. Marking its position on a stick before he sailed would allow him to check his latitude in relation to his port of sailing, but this was less use than one might at first expect with 24 hours of daylight around midsummer in high northern latitudes. An Icelander nicknamed 'Star-Oddi' actually produced a set of latitude tables for various stars (including the sun) in the tenth century.

It is also possible that a type of Calcite found on an island in Oslofjord has the property of polarising light. The author has a piece of this rock and it is true that one face will turn pale blue when turned in the hand on a cloudy day. A little common sense observation will then allow one to determine approximately where the sun is even when obscured by cloud. The earliest secure reference we have for this is in the thirteenth century, but the sagas tell us that a Viking king was using a 'sun stone' to navigate his ship in the eleventh century.

Although the Drakkars (as the big warships were called) were normally only used for fairly local voyages, it was not impossible for the largest warships to travel great distances. One of the wrecks in the Roskilde Ship Museum found at Skudulev known as Wreck One, was a warship estimated at or near 100ft long (30m). For a long time it was thought to have been a locally-built vessel until the advent of dendrochronology (the science of tree-ring dating). This analysis showed that the oak timbers for the vessel came from Ireland.

Long and narrow and frequently over 100ft (30m) long, the hulls must have warped and twisted with every wave. Even on a smaller ship this can be witnessed by the crew as

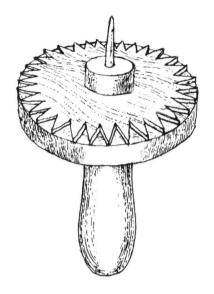

86 A sun compass based upon an imcomplete example found in Greenland

the bowpost and sternposts move out of alignment as the ship ripples forwards over the peaks and troughs of the waves. A large storm could break the vessel's back. The art would have been to hug the coast, visiting friendly ports along the way, hopping across the more open stretches on good sailing days. In ideal conditions, Denmark is at least three whole days sail away from England, and often longer. There was a term that meant literally 'A good days sailing' and this was used to describe the estimated distance of 150 miles (241km) at sea.

As an example, the famous Gokstad ship, and the various replica versions that have sailed since the hull was discovered at the end of the nineteenth century, have demonstrated that the ship requires about 10 tonnes of ballast, with the ship weighing in at 20 tonnes unladen. With all this, she drew only 3ft of water, and even then, she could carry another 10 tonnes and still only draw an extra foot.

Pressures of profit may have encouraged the trader's steersman to take risks and overload the ship with more than was safe to carry. Any passengers had to be patient, something we do not really understand today with scheduled services. There were no timetables as such, just better times to sail in than others. This also had an effect on when the raiding season began. Over winter, the Viking ships crews, as can be read in the Anglo-Saxon Chronicles, often laid-up in winter camps. Cnut's army did just this in AD 1014 for instance.

If the wind was not blowing mainly in the direction you needed to go, it was common sense to stay in port. The crews in a warship could row against the wind, but without a driving need to be somewhere at a particular time, it was just too much like hard work. A trader would have only used oar power to pull out into the clearway so as to catch the wind and would never have rowed far. Even if the wind direction was good, but overall conditions were too rough, you stayed in port. Without any night vision devices or lighthouses, sailing close inshore at night was foolish. The traveller was at the behest of many forces and may have had to wait a long time for all the right factors to come together.

Whilst the men in the warship would probably have had other ships in the fleet and men to reassure each other when they reached England, the men in the trader were entirely on their own, with just their wits to defend themselves. It is impossible for us today to really understand the risks and surprises that the Viking traders must have endured, although the Saxon poem *The Seafarer* gives a few clues.

Even though the Vikings were sometimes called pirates by the Anglo-Saxons, they were subject to just the same problems out of home waters. Pirates across the ages have by and large followed the same plan. Once you have selected your target, approach with

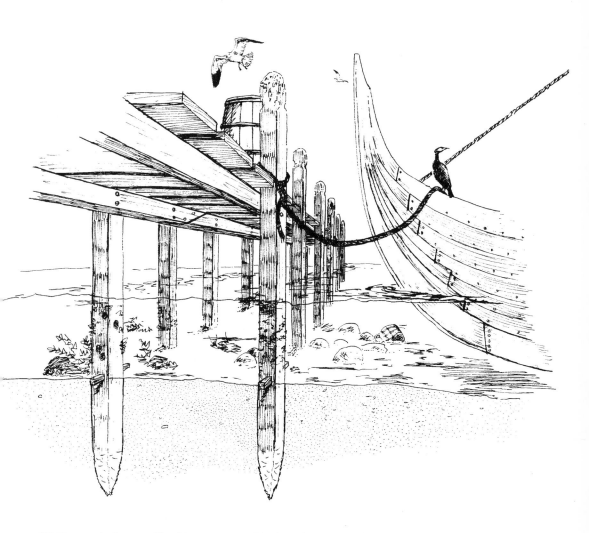

87 Purpose-built quays like this were unusual in the Viking Age and many ships would either have been beached to be unloaded and goods carried ashore or transferred to other boats

88 *Encountering a Dhow. Taking their ships into waters far from home brought Norse shipwrights into contact with other, older traditions*

stealth, and try to appear innocuous. At the last moment, speed up in your smaller but swifter craft and overrun the target. Once contact is made, overwhelm your opposition with extreme force, as they will be largely unarmed and few in number. The only option for the trader is to avoid being seen (which is a matter of luck), by sailing well offshore. Poor weather will also help as the pirates are unlikely to have such durable vessels. It would seem to our Anglo-Saxon minds ironic for Vikings to become slaves themselves, which undoubtedly occurred.

Not all other vessels in the Mediterranean were pirates, even if the trader's crew were jumpy enough to believe so. The Arab nations plied the Mediterranean far more often than the Vikings. They too suffered from pirates, so that when vessels from both sides of Europe 'bumped' into each other, the crews if they had never seen the likes of their various ships would have been very alarmed. The Arab 'Dhow' (technically called a 'Boom') would sport a variety of different construction techniques, sail and rigging styles that the Vikings, if they had picked up on them, would have altered their sailing abilities for the better. It carries a Lateen rig or sail which is excellent for sailing into the wind in combination with the bow-sprit or jib. This means that even when the wind was blowing in largely the opposite direction that you desired to sail in, you could still make some headway even though it was slow work. The Boom carries two masts, nearly doubling the efficiency of the sail area. The jib-boom on the nose also carried extra sail, even though the ship was not vastly longer than the Knarr. The cargo hold was huge, and was virtually enclosed, not an open boat such as the Knarr. And most obvious, it uses a rudder that sits at the rear or stern of the ship, a vastly superior method of control. If they ever got the chance to talk to the Arab captain or 'Mallah', they may have picked up some superior methods of navigating as well. The Arabs had the advantage of geographical and historical proximity to the Greeks, and it was the Greeks who pioneered modern methods of navigating by calculation rather than by dead reckoning. The lodestone or magnet was one such example. The kind of ore that attracted iron was once called magnesian stone, because it was discovered in the part of Asia Minor near Magnesia. The name of the ore came into English as magnet.

The discovery of the magnet's use in determining direction seems to have been made independently in China and Europe certainly before the twelfth century. If a bit of magnetised iron was allowed to float freely on a stick in water, it consistently pointed in a north-south direction. In the late twelfth century an English theologian and natural philosopher named Alexander Neckam suggested the potential use of magnets for navigation. Soon afterwards the magnetic compass was devised as an aid to sailors.

Other instruments that Arab navigators used at this time were the cross-staff and the astrolabe, two devices that the Greeks had invented to measure the altitudes of celestial bodies. From these measurements it was possible to determine the approximate latitude of the vessel as well as approximate local time. The simplest version of the cross-staff was a stick, or staff, about 3ft (0.9m) long with a shorter sliding stick set at right angles to the staff. The navigator pointed the staff at a spot about halfway between the horizon and the sun or a star. The crosspiece was then moved until the sights at its ends were in line with both the observed body and the horizon. A scale along the staff showed the altitude, or angle above the horizon, of the body. It is difficult to use on a heaving deck and eye injuries were common.

The astrolabe was a disk of brass or bronze, 4-20in (10-50cm) in diameter. A pointer, called an alidade, was pivoted at the centre of the disk. One person held the astrolabe by a small ring at the top while another person knelt facing the rim of the instrument. The person kneeling pointed the alidade at the sun or a star and read the angle from the markings on the disk. From these readings, calculations could be made to determine the ship's position. However, the key to all these innovations was the written word and the chart on which you plotted your course. Neither of which the Vikings used — with the exception of Runes — and with Runes, you could not calculate short of simple mental reckoning. And to compound the problem, the Vikings as a rule couldn't read, let alone understand Arabic. Not that any of these unrealised setbacks prevented the Vikings from sailing nearly everywhere in Europe, the Mediterranean, and crossing the Atlantic, all of which are well documented elsewhere.

Only a few years ago, a replica Knarr was sailed around the world by a Norwegian crew. The weather however does not re-enact, and in 1997, the Knarr and an Oseberg replica were lost at sea in the Bay of Biscay.

Anyone who has handled even the simplest sailing vessel will readily empathize with these men who had but a three-inch plank between them and eternity. The living heave of the deck beneath one's feet, the thrum of the water along the strakes, the burr of vibration through the tiller bar and the steadily rising note of the wind in the rigging as the good ship shoulders the green sea aside. None of these things have changed and the exhilaration of being out in 'a good blow' would only be increased by knowing that soon you would be a stranger in a strange land, fighting with friends against the Saxons for land or silver. Perhaps even the old Gods of Asgard will smile on you on such a pleasant spring day as you turn your shoulder toward home. One day, the lucky ones will be back, richer, wiser and older, but for now the whole world is waiting for them.

Glossary

Aback	with the wind thrusting the ship backwards
Abaft	from behind
After castle	a work in wood having a castle-like appearance on the stern part of a ship
Alidade	a revolving index for reading the graduations of an astrolabe, quadrant or similar instrument
Astrolabe	an archaic instrument used for taking the altitude of a star etc.
Aventail	in the context of this book, the skirt of mail at the back of a helmet
Bast	a fibre made from the phloem of birch bark. Can be woven into coarse cloth or made up into ropes
Blind ended	a hole with a bottom
Bowpost	the foremost timber in a ship — an extension of the keel
Bow-sprit	a spar of wood jutting forward from the bows of a ship
Butt ended	a joint in woodwork where two flat ends of a plank abut one another
Cabe/rowlock	a thorn-shaped piece of grown timber attached to the top edge of the gunwale to which one attaches an oar
Cleat	a double horn-shaped piece of wood to which sailing ropes are attached
Clinker-built	a method of ship construction where each successive plank is attached to the top edge of the preceding plank
Cog	the large ship of burden or war that replaced the Longship type in northern Europe
Conning	sailing the ship and having command of the vessel
Crossbeam	a beam below deck level that crosses the ship from side to side
Cross-sea	a description of the wave state when at 90 degrees to the line of sailing
Drakkar	a Viking warship of 100ft in length or more
Endpost	also stern post. The aftmost timber in a ship — an extension of the keel
Forecastle	a work in wood having a castle-like appearance on the bows part of a ship
Freeboard	literally, the amount of the side of the ship free of the sea
Gangplank	a sturdy plank, often equipped with cross pieces, along which one can walk from the ship to the land. From the Old Norse 'Ganga' — to walk

Garboard Strake	the plank forming part of the side of the ship that is directly connected to the side of the keel
Gunwale	literally 'gun-wall', the side of the ship above the upper deck
Jib	a triangular sail carried in front of the mast
Keelson	a heavy timber cut so as to fit across the bottom of a ship of the Longship type that accepts the foot of the mast and spreads the loads there from across a substantial part of the keel
Knees	grown timbers specially shaped and fixed to the gunwale and deck to transfer bending stresses
Lateen	a triangular sail common in Mediterranean vessels
Rove	a square nail driven through the timbers of a clinker built vessel and having a round-holed washer driven down its shaft before the end is peened over
Roving	the act of fastening roving nails
Samson post	strong vertical posts well affixed at the sides of a ship and used for hauling ropes around, mooring etc.
Scarf joint	a joint in woodwork where the abutting ends of two pieces of wood are shaped so as to bring them smoothly together without a change of section
Scend	the carry of the waves: literally, to pitch into the trough of a wave
Sheets	the ropes attached to the corners of a sail by which the attitude of the sail may be adjusted in relation to the wind
Starboard	the right-hand side of the ship when standing aft and facing forward. Literally, 'steer board' in respect of a vessel with a side rudder
Sternpost	see endpost
Strake	a plank used in the construction of the sides of a clinker-built vessel
Tack	an alternate course in zigzag; the act of sailing a vessel across the eye of the wind; the lower windward corner of a sail; the rope attached to that corner
Thwarts	an above-deck beam or plank stretching across a ship or boat. Particularly, a beam used as a rowing bench
Tiller	a rudder in common parlance, but actually the bar set at 90 degrees to the rudder by which the rudder is moved
Transom	the flat end at the stern of vessels not of the Longship type
Virgins / 'angels' / 'maidens'	a descriptive term used by Norse sailors to describe the flat block of wood used as a pulley block in sailing terms
Weregild	a fine by which homicide and other heinous crimes might be expiated
Whale	a shaped timber fixed to the ship at deck level on some mid-period vessels of the Longship type. It helps to spread the thrust from the mast at deck level
Yard or yardarm	the horizontal timber that carries the sail

Bibliography

Note: This bibliography is by no means exhaustive and indicates those books which the author has found interesting and relevant to the subject over the last few years

Abels, Richard, *Alfred the Great — War, Kingship and Culture in Anglo-Saxon England*. Addison Wesley Longman Ltd, Harlow. ISBN 0 5820 4048 5 CSD

Allen Brown, R., *The Norman Conquest of England*. Boydell & Brewer Ltd, Suffolk. ISBN 0 8511 5618 5

Arwidsson, Greta, 'Schilde'. In: G. Arwidsson (Ed.), *Birka II: Systematische Analysen der GrSberfunde, vol. 2*. KVHAA: Stockholm, 1986

Bersu, Gerhardt & Wilson, David M., 'Three Viking graves in the Isle of Man'. *Society for Medieval Archaeology, monograph 1*. Society for Medieval Archaeology: London, 1966

Dickinson, Tania & Herke, Heinrich, *Early Anglo-Saxon shields, Archaeologica 110*, Society of Antiquaries of London: London, 1992

Ellis-Davidson, Hilda, *The Sword in Anglo-Saxon England*. Boydell & Brewer Ltd, Suffolk. ISBN 0 8511 5716 X

Evans, Stephen, *The Lords of Battle*. Boydell & Brewer Ltd, Suffolk. IP12 3DF. ISBN 0 8511 5662 2

Griffith, Paddy, *The Viking Art of War*. Greenhill Books, London. 1995

Hagen, Ann, *A Handbook of Anglo-Saxon Food. Processing and Consumption*. Anglo-Saxon Books, Norfolk. ISBN 0 9516 2098 3

Hatto, A.T. (trans.), *The Nibelungenlied*. Penguin Classics

Hawkes, Jane, & Mills, Susan (ed), *Northumbria's Golden Age*. Sutton Publishing Ltd, Stroud. ISBN 0 7509 1685 0

Haywood, John, *Dark Age Naval Power*. Anglo-Saxon Books, Norfolk, ISBN 1 8982 8122 X

Heaney, Seamus (trans.), *BEOWULF: A New Translation*. Faber/Penguin,
    ISBN 0 1418 0123 X

Henson, Donald, *A Guide to Late Anglo-Saxon England*. Anglo-Saxon Books, Norfolk.
    ISBN 1 8982 8121 1

Herbert, Kathleen, *Spellcraft. Old English Heroic Legends*. Anglo-Saxon Books, Norfolk.
    ISBN 0 9516 2099 1

Higham, N.J., *The Death of Anglo-Saxon England*. Sutton Publishing Ltd, Stroud.
    ISBN 0 7509 0885 8

Howarth, David, *1066: The Year of the Conquest*. William Collins & Sons Ltd, London

Hutchinson, Gillian, *Medieval Ships and Shipping*. Leicester University Press, London.
    ISBN 0 7185 0117 9

Jesch, Judith, *Women in the Viking Age*. Boydell & Brewer Ltd, Suffolk. ISBN 0 8511 5360 7

Keys, David, *Catastrophe*. Century, Random House, UK

Lacey, Robert & Danziger, Danny, *The Year 1000*. Little, Brown & Co., London.
    ISBN 0 3166 4375 0

Lawson, M.K., *Cnut*. Longman Group ltd, Harlow. ISBN 0 5820 5969 0 CSD

Logan, F. Donald, *The Vikings in History*. Hutchinson, London. ISBN 0 4150 8396 6

Marsden, John, *The Fury of the Northmen*. Kyle Cathie Ltd, London. ISBN 1 8562 6236 7

Morillo, Stephen, *The Battle of Hastings*. Boydell & Brewer Ltd, Woodbridge.
    ISBN 0 8511 5619 3

Nicolaysen, N., *The Viking ship discovered at Gokstad in Norway*. Christiana: Oslo, 1882.
    Reprinted: Gregg International Publ.: Westmead UK, 1971

Oakeshott, Ewart, *Dark Age Warrior*. Lutterworth Press, London. ISBN 0 7188 2079 7

Oakeshott, Ewart, *Records of the Medieval Sword*. The Boydell Press, Suffolk. 1991,
    reprinted 1998. Available from Book Club Associates, Swindon and other sources

Oakshott, Ewart, *The Sword in the Age of Chivalry*. Published by Boydell & Brewer Ltd,
    Suffolk. ISBN 0 8511 5715 7

Oakshott, Ewart, *The Archaeology of Weapons*. Boydell & Brewer Ltd, Woodbridge. ISBN 0 8511 5738 6

Owen, Olwyn & Dalland, Magnar, *Scar: A Viking Boat Burial on Sanday, Orkney*. Tuckwell Press, East Linton. ISBN 0 8623 2080

Peddie, John, *Alfred — Warrior King*. Sutton Publishing Ltd, Stroud

Pollington, Stephen, *An Introduction to the Old English Language and its Literature*. Anglo-Saxon Books, Norfolk. ISBN 1 8982 8106 8

Pollington, Stephen, *The English Warrior*. Anglo-Saxon Books, Norfolk. ISBN 1 8982 8110 6

Pollington, Stephen, *Rudiments of Runelore*. Anglo-Saxon Books, Norfolk. ISBN 1 8982 8116 5

Pollington, Stephen, *Wordcraft. A Concise Dictionary & Thesaurus*. Anglo-Saxon Books, Norfolk. ISBN 1 8982 8102 5

Porter, John (trans.), *Anglo-Saxon Riddles*. Anglo-Saxon Books, Norfolk. ISBN 1 8982 8113 0

Shadrake, Dan & Susanna, *Barbarian Warriors — Saxons, Vikings and Normans*. 144pp, 150+ colour photos, line drawings and B&Ws. Brasseys

Smiley, Jane (ed.) *The Sagas of the Icelanders*. Allen Lane at the Penguin Press, London. Available from Book Club Associates

Snyder, Christopher A., *An Age of Tyrants*. Sutton Publishing Ltd, Stroud. ISBN 0 7509 1929 9

Tolkien, J.R.R., *The Homecoming of Beorhtnoth*. Anglo-Saxon Books, Norfolk

Tweddle, Dominic, *The Anglian Helmet From Coppergate*. Council for British Archaeology, 112, Kennington Road, London. SE11 6RE for the York Archaeological Trust. Volume 17 in the 'Small finds' series. ISBN 1 8724 1419 2

Underwood, Richard, *Anglo–Saxon Weapons and Warfare*. Tempus Publishing Ltd, Stroud. ISBN 0 7524 1412 7

Warren Hollister, C., *Anglo-Saxon Military Institutions on the eve of the Norman Conquest*. Oxford University Press, Oxford. ISBN 0 1982 1296 8

The Anglo Saxons. CD-ROM disk by RM Learning Resources, Oxford in association with the British Museum

The Icelandic Sagas. Orkneyinga Saga, Egil's Saga, the Vinland Saga, Njal's Saga, Laxdaela Saga (Penguin Classics series), Jhomsvikinga Saga (University of Texas Press), Grettir the Strong (University of Toronto Press)

The Norwegian Invasion of England in 1066 by Kelly DeVries. Boydell & Brewer Ltd, PO Box 9, Woodbridge, Suffolk. IP12 3DF. ISBN 0 85115 763 7

Further information

Britain has been called 'an offshore museum, conveniently moored within a short distance of the western European seaboard'. Certainly, the British people have a very strong sense of their history and preserving our heritage — or at least the physical traces of it — has become big business.

Regia Anglorum, 9, Durleigh Close, Bristol. BS13 7NQ.
Website, http://www.regia.org

Regia Anglorum are specifically interested in the recreation of the life and times of the people who lived in and around the British Isles between the reigns of Alfred the Great and Richard the Lionheart, AD 850-1150. Founded in 1986 with the particular aim of forwarding the *authentic* recreation of Britain's history, they have done much to concentrate the minds of other re-enactors. Regia have five full-scale ship replicas, a large living history encampment and perform major battle re-enactments. Always at the cutting edge of physical reconstructions, they are constructing a permanent site in Kent covering two acres that will represent a Manorial Burgh, a defended longhall and other buildings.

Jorvik Viking Centre, Coppergate, York. Yorkshire. YO1 1NT.
Website, http://www.jorvik-viking-centre.co.uk

The Jorvik Viking Centre is the premier visitor attraction dealing with the Viking Age in the Britain. Fully revised at a cost of £4.2m in the winter of 2000/2001, this hugely popular centre in the middle of York is based upon the real buildings in which the Vikings lived. Travelling into the city from the river Foss, the visitor is carried through backyards and alleyways, through the upper storey of a house and on to Coppergate in the heart of the Viking trading metropolis of AD 975.

The English Companions, 38, Cranworth Rd, Worthing. BN11 2JF.
Website, http://www.kami.demon.co.uk/gesithas/

Whilst not a re-enactment society, The English Companions is exclusively devoted to Anglo-Saxon history. Its aims are to bring together all those with an interest in the language, culture and traditions of Anglo-Saxon England and to promote a wider interest in, and knowledge of, all things Anglo-Saxon. The Fellowship publishes a journal, *Widowinde*, which enables members to keep in touch with current thinking on a wide range of associated topics. The *Gesithas* enables like-minded people to keep in contact by publicising conferences, courses and meetings that might be of interest to its members. A correspondence course in Old English is also available.

NAReS, PO Box 1812, Swindon, Wiltshire. SN2 6AY.
Website, http://www.nares.org

If you are interested in becoming involved at any level, there is almost certainly a specialist group that shares your interest. The National Association of Re-enactment Societies (NAReS) acts in the manner of a professional body and represents the interests of the British re-enactor. It principally interacts with government bodies, the police etc. and has done much to ameliorate legislation that would otherwise have made the pursuit of this pastime virtually impossible. They do not accept individual members but can suggest which societies might interest the aspiring recreator of history.

English Heritage, Special Events Unit, 23, Saville Row, London W1X 1AB.
Website, http://www.english-heritage.org.uk

There is a continuing interest in re-enactment in the UK and perhaps 25,000 people are actively involved in the hobby. The single largest employers of re-enactors in the UK, English Heritage has done more than most to ensure that a visit to a historic property during the summer months will ensure you see a living demonstration of some aspect of our history.

Index

Page numbers in **bold** refer to illustrations